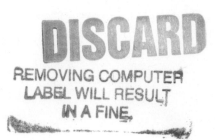

Praise for *But Now I See*

"Steven is a class act, and his story is one of perseverance. I am lucky to have heard it from Steven himself, just as you will in these pages. The Olympic Movement is a movement about friendship, excellence, and respect, and you will see those values very clearly in Steven's story."

—SCOTT BLACKMUN, CEO, U.S. Olympic Committee

"Steven Holcomb's vision of a goal was not only seen with the eyes, but also with his heart! As you will read in *But Now I See*, true champions always find a way to win."

—RICHARD H. WRIGHT, President/CEO, AdvoCare

But Now I See

MY JOURNEY FROM BLINDNESS TO OLYMPIC GOLD

STEVEN HOLCOMB

WITH STEVE EUBANKS

BENBELLA BOOKS, INC.
DALLAS, TEXAS

BenBella

BenBella Books, Inc.
10300 N. Central Expressway, Suite 400
Dallas, TX 75231
www.benbellabooks.com
Send feedback to feedback@benbellabooks.com

Printed in the United States of America

10 9 8 7 6 5 4 3 2

Library of Congress Cataloging-in-Publication Data is available for this title.
978-1-9378-5600-7

Edited by Debbie Harmsen
Copyediting by Lisa Miller and Stacia Seaman
Proofreading by Chris Gage, James Fraleigh, and Thuy Vo
Cover design by Sarah Dombrowsky
Cover photo courtesy of Getty Images
Text design and composition by Neuwirth & Associates, Inc.
Printed by Bang Printing

Distributed by Perseus Distribution
(www.perseusdistribution.com)

To place orders through Perseus Distribution:
Tel: (800) 343-4499
Fax: (800) 351-5073
E-mail: orderentry@perseusbooks.com

Significant discounts for bulk sales are available. Please contact Glenn Yeffeth at glenn@benbellabooks.com or (214) 750-3628.

To my mom and dad, for working so hard to give me every opportunity possible and always believing in me

Contents

Foreword

Ever since I was a boy in Chemung, New York, I have loved the thrill of racing. My family owned the town racetrack, and I was on it by about the same time I learned to tie my shoes. Fast cars, from hot rods to stock cars, just get me going. I love to be behind the wheel, and I also love watching racing. I'm a huge fan.

In 1992 I watched a different kind of race, bobsledding in the Winter Olympics. I was enthralled—and then appalled when I learned that no bobsleds were Made in the USA. We had to get ours from Europe and they were inferior to the sleds used by the other teams. I was outraged when I saw that the sleds were affecting our performance. How could Team USA not have equipment made in America?

After discussions with the USA Bobsled and Skeleton Federation and riding in a bobsled myself, I founded Bo-Dyn and worked with Bob Cuneo, the owner of Chassis Dynamics, to make a top-notch sled for our team. We didn't know what we were doing and were pressed for time. But we worked long and hard. We learned how bobsleds work, what makes them go fast, what feels right to the athletes. We built a sled that wasn't like anyone else's. And at the 2010 Olympics in Vancouver, Steven Holcomb drove The Night Train, built by our Bo-Dyn team, to gold medal victory.

Standing near the finish line as Steven and his team completed their Olympic journey of being 2010 Olympic four-man bobsled gold medal champions, and being the founder of the Bo-Dyn Bobsled Project, I understood how blessed I am to be an American and to have met the man Steven Holcomb. Steven put his country first in his life and first on the Olympic podium. Steven's courage and determination, which has guided him through his personal life and athletic life, demonstrates that he has the "heart of a champion."

Reading this account about the segment of Steven's life that took him to becoming an Olympic bobsled gold medal winner has inspired me to appreciate his dedication to the sport, and I hope it will inspire you to reach out and support the Olympic Movement that men and women around the world are a part of.

Geoff Bodine
NASCAR Champion and Founder of
Bo-Dyn Bobsled Project

But Now I See

Prologue

tanding on the ice of the bobsled sliding track before the most important run of my life, I welcome fear like an old friend, and I know my three teammates feel the same way. We are at the 2010 Vancouver Olympic Games, and it is intense. All four of us shake our hands in the air as if we've touched a hot plate. One of my teammates rolls his head from side to side like a fighter before the start of a round, and we bounce on our toes to burn off nervous energy. This lasts only a couple of seconds, but it feels longer. Time passes slowly and quietly once I burrow deep into the mental rabbit hole that athletes call "the zone." There are hundreds of screaming fans nearby, thousands in the stands, and more along the length of the sliding track, but the place might as well be empty. The cheers are like white noise. Every muscle is taut, every nerve is on edge. This is it.

We press the heels of our spiked shoes on the two-inch wooden block that passes as a starting line, and I crouch into a standing sprinter's stance, loading all my energy into my glutes and quads. There is a verbal cadence, like a countdown, that establishing of a rhythm so we can explode in sync toward the sled. I finally take a few deep breaths as the cadence begins.

My teammates and I haven't been silent, but we don't need to share our feelings either. We all know the stakes. Six seconds from now we will be loaded in the sled that I will pilot down one of the most dangerous tracks in Olympic history.

I drive The Night Train, an intimidating, flat black, four-man bobsled loosely named after a Harley-Davidson motorcycle that screams "badass." It is already the most famous bobsled in the world, one that has sparked all kinds of crazy rumors about secret metal compounds and paints developed by NASA. We don't discourage such talk; in fact, we do what we can to foster it. There's nothing wrong with setting up rent-free residency in your opponents' heads, which is what we've done by staying quiet and letting the rumors fly. Now, with the words "USA-1" painted on its nose, The Night Train looks fast even when it's sitting still.

Every run begins from a dead stop. Our only propulsion comes from gravity and the initial force the four of us exert through pushing, which will start in less than a second. We've made only about forty runs on this track, not a big number for an Olympic venue, but the Canadians decided early on to limit access—a smart move from a competitive standpoint, but one that has earned them a lot of criticism as the Vancouver Olympic Games have progressed. Bobsledding, luge, and skeleton use the same track. Those are, perhaps, the only Olympic sports where the host nation has a decided home-field advantage. The Canadian hockey team has the roaring support of the fans, but the dimensions of the rink aren't changed to suit the team. The nets are the same size and the blue lines are in the same place as in every other hockey rink. The same is true in figure skating, half-pipe snowboarding, swimming, tennis, and basketball: the home team might have the crowd on its side, but the playing field isn't customized to benefit one team over another.

That is not the case in bobsledding. There is no set configuration for a sliding track, so each course has its own layout and style. The track in St. Moritz, Switzerland, is a steady, steep drop with sweeping turns that don't slow you down, while the track in Lake Placid, New York, is steep but slow because of the configuration of the turns. The track in Whistler is steep in the beginning and then levels off before getting steep again near the bottom, where the most treacherous turns are found. That wouldn't be a problem if every team had gotten equal access to the track so we could all figure it out. But the Canadians instituted a program called "Own the Podium" by which they restricted access for everyone but their teams. There were times when we couldn't even look at the track. So while I've had forty runs here, the Canadians have made more than a hundred. And in a sport where repetition is crucial to confidence, and confidence crucial to speed, we are at a decided disadvantage, one that only heightens the anxiety.

There is a lot to be scared of on this track. A Georgian luger, Nodar Kumaritashvili, was killed during a practice run just prior to the opening ceremony. A dozen bobsled crashes followed, including one by the German women's team where the brakeman was thrown onto the track. Australia had to withdraw from the four-man competition after its driver and brakeman suffered concussions during a crash, and the Dutch team pulled out because its driver, Edwin van Calker, admitted to being too scared to continue. "For me, it's not about competing; it's about surviving," Edwin told the media afterward.

None of that enters my mind now. I've been here several hundred times in my mind already, visualizing the lines for each turn and imagining every second of a perfect run. Nothing shy of perfection will do. The Germans, the dominant team in bobsledding, have finished their fourth and final run and are watching us from a viewing area at the bottom. One slight bobble during our run and the Germans will win.

As the reigning World Champion, I'm accustomed to that kind of pressure. Whether it's a gold medal run in front of a cheering crowd or a practice run with no one around, the reality remains the same: one wrong move at ninety miles an hour and somebody's going to the hospital, or worse. Not only do I embrace the weight of that reality, I love every second of it. I love the discipline and teamwork it takes to guide this projectile down a steep sheet of ice, where a tenth of a second can mean the difference between finishing first or fifth; the strength and speed needed to push a four-hundred-pound sled fifty meters in five seconds, and then jump into it without jostling or slowing it down; the experience required to guide that sled through curves where my teammates and I pull six g's, six times our body weight and twice the force astronauts experience during a Space Shuttle launch: those are the things that get my heart pumping. When I no longer feel the tingle on my skin and the twinge in my gut—the second those fear receptors shut down and I say, "Ho hum, another run"—that is the day I'll call it quits.

We start. I sprint to the push bar at the front of the sled. My teammates hit their marks as well. Shouts of "Go! Go! Go!" shower in from both sides of the starting line, and some enthusiastic fan in the crowd clangs a cowbell like a tambourine.

As is the case with a lot of Winter Olympic sports, the average person on the street watches bobsledding once, maybe twice, every four years, depending on if the World Championships are televised at a convenient time. From a spectator standpoint, bobsledding (or "bobsleighing" as it's called everywhere but the United States) isn't that difficult to figure out: teams push sleds from a dead stop and jump in. The driver pilots the sled down the track through lots of scary turns at high speeds. The fastest team wins. Someone who has never seen a bobsled race can watch for about thirty seconds and figure it out. But since bobsledding is not a traditional American sport, most USA fans take only a passing interest. When Jamaica put a team on the ice for the first time at Calgary, Canada, in 1988, people pulled for them out of curiosity and admiration (the movie *Cool Runnings* came from it), and when NFL and track stars like Herschel Walker and Edwin Moses try their hands at pushing, Americans watch. We get some people who watch because it's the Olympics and others who watch because it's a race and they would watch lawnmower racing if it were televised.

Some people, however, watch because bobsledding is dangerous. Crashes happen, even among the best in the world. Like they do with NASCAR and professional bull riding, some casual viewers tune in to see the wrecks. But bobsled athletes are not daredevils. When done correctly, a great bobsledding run is a finely choreographed, physically demanding work of art that requires strength, speed, explosiveness, and years of practice to master.

That's where we are now. One-point-one seconds in and we're at full sprint.

Behind me, Steve Mesler, Curtis Tomasevicz, and Justin Olsen, powerful men who would look just as at home on an NFL sideline or in a UFC cage as they do on the ice, push as hard and fast as they can. To the casual observer, this is four guys charging headlong down the ice like weightlifters pushing a buddy's broken car. In fact, the first seconds of a run are a ballet, each step precisely timed and balanced so that we get not only a fast start but also a clean start. We have practiced this precise start thousands of times, sometimes on a track and many more times on a flat surface. The timing is down to the millisecond, and the balance of the push is exact so that neither side is pushed harder than the other.

Think of a bobsled run as being like a car hitting a patch of ice on the highway. We have grooves cut into the track at the start to keep the sled moving straight (it would be impossible to push the sled straight without them), but still, you have little traction and even less friction. In the first 1.5 seconds of a run, the push athletes get The Night Train moving as fast as possible toward a sheer sheet of ice. At 2.1 seconds I jump into the sled, sliding my legs into the nose and getting low enough to eliminate aerodynamic drag. Everything is about shaving hundredths of seconds off our time. Bobsled runners are not blades like you find on kids' sleds hanging in garages. They are rounded like the cross-section of a steel pipe. This cuts down on drag, but it also makes steering a bit challenging. That's my job: drive this sled on the fastest lines possible, getting us to the bottom of the track in the quickest time (and in one piece). But instead of a steering wheel, I'm controlling the front runners through a couple of ropes with D-rings on the end. Pull the left ring and the sled turns left and the right ring pulls the sled right, although if you've ever turned the steering wheel of your car when you're skidding on ice, you understand how tenuous that can be. Now imagine your car on a patch of ice that is a mile long, downhill, with fourteen turns. That is a bobsled run.

My teammates load into the sled at closer to the three-second mark than four. We're known for our "clean" loads, which means my teammates and I get into the sled without slowing it down. This is no easy feat. Most people would get into a moving sled by pulling on the nearest handle. That, of course, would slow the sled down. Since I'm already seated, any pull, no matter how slight, will jerk my head forward, and I'll know instantly that we just slowed down; so having a clean run is that much more important. My team doesn't drag us often anymore, but it does happen occasionally. Not this time. This load is one of our cleanest. We hit the first time mark in 4.76 seconds—a great start.

All in, the clock rolls past five seconds.

From this moment forward, the success or failure of the run is up to the driver—me. The push athletes share the risk, certainly, but from here on out they are passengers. Oddly, I'm calmer now than I was before the run began, even though the danger is more immediate. My heart is beating slower and steadier, and the fear has dissipated. I'm in my routine. As important and life altering as the next thirty seconds will be, I am experiencing what researchers call "expectant euphoria." My blood pressure and cortisol levels drop even though the stresses on the body and mind are at their peak. Calm settles over me as we pick up speed and head into the first turn, just as I have visualized. There have been plenty of scientific studies to explain why this happens, but for me the answer is simple: as treacherous and taxing as the next few seconds will be, I am in control. Fear flies out the back of the sled once the action begins. The crowd, the Germans, the gold medal—all those thoughts are gone. I am, at this moment, completely at peace because our destiny is in my hands . . .

ONE
Blinding Fear

Fear is the most intense, stimulating high a human can experience. Nothing else comes close. From the "startle reflex"—that dilating and widening of the eyes and tightening of the muscles that comes about when your car hits a slick spot or someone sneaks up behind you and yells "Boo!"—to the off-the-charts heartbeats—the quick breathing, the adrenal gland in overdrive, and the sharpened senses as blood flees certain organs and rushes to major muscle groups—no drug can replicate the feeling of dozens of hormones flooding the body and billions of cells firing in response to fear. It is a reflex triggered deep inside the amygdala, a section of the brain near the cerebral cortex, one that causes you to tighten your face and duck your head when firecrackers go off close to you or when the scary monster jumps out in a movie. It is why women are able to lift cars off trapped children and arthritic old men are able to beat off young muggers.

This adrenaline rush is the reason some people jump off cliffs wearing wing suits or somersault off the Eiffel Tower holding their parachutes in their hands. It is why people line up for roller coasters, or strap bungee cords to their legs, or go off-trail to create their own ski runs. Despite your logical brain screaming for you to flee from such dangers, fear packs an intoxicating lure. The successful television show *Fear Factor* was created around the idea that people will do incredible things once immersed in the emotion of fear. The rush makes you forget the mundane problems of life. You become totally immersed in now.

Great athletes know the sensation better than most. That instant before the football is snapped, amid the yelling and shifting and watching as the man in front of you prepares to hurl his body at you with all the force he can muster, those precious seconds create a feeling that is unmatched—and irreplaceable. Many professional football players struggle and flounder in their personal lives after leaving the game. Former Tampa Bay Buccaneers star Kevin Carter told me, "Every NFL player has trouble coming down off the high after leaving the league. Some handle it better than others, but every player feels it."

BUT NOW I SEE

It's why Herschel Walker, a successful businessman in the food industry, became a mixed martial arts fighter, and why Chad Ochocinco chose to ride a bull and wrestle an alligator during the brief NFL lockout. It's also why boxers seem to always stay in the ring one fight too long and why race car drivers continue to compete well into their forties. The high is incredibly addictive.

Some people call it "butterflies" or "jitters," but whatever the name, the same physiology defines it. Epinephrine and norepinephrine cause the skin to constrict and the glucose levels in the blood to increase. Arteries and veins expand to increase blood flow, nostrils flare, and lung capacity increases. That chemical reaction is why a champion skier can be sweating like crazy in the starting gate even though it's freezing outside and why a sprinter can get chills on a ninety-degree afternoon as he puts his feet on the starting block. No matter how many times an athlete has been called on to make the crucial final play, that hair-on-the-arms feeling and churn in the pit of the stomach never goes away. Athletes call it something else—"nerves" perhaps, because no champion will use the "F" word—but the autonomic responses don't lie: their bodies are responding to fear.

For as long as I can remember, I've had a healthy working relationship with fear. My father had me on skis before I was fully potty trained, and I raced the slopes of Park City, Utah, long before I could read or write. When I was four years old, I was going off-trail, weaving through the trees and finding my own way, much to the horror of my mother, who was an intermediate skier and always rushing to catch up. The faster I got, the more challenging the runs became. Rarely did I glide leisurely down the mountain. Every run was about going a little faster. Crashing only served as a reminder that this wasn't badminton. Snow, ice, and steep slopes are the most inhospitable environments humans encounter this side of outer space. Preparation with a pinch of fear keeps you sharp, especially when sliding down a run.

Throughout my brief competitive skiing career, I was always trying to push the limits. Could I take a straighter downhill line? Could I get closer to the gates? Could I get lower, streamline my body to make myself more aerodynamic? Could I squeeze a tenth of a second off an already breakneck run? But all those questions were really asking the same thing: could I stare fear in the face without flinching?

I haven't discussed any of this with my teammates because it's not necessary, and talking about such things is not what athletes do. If you go into a team locker room before a championship game, you don't hear guys talking about fear or what they are feeling. Most athletes say nothing, preferring to prepare in the serenity of silence. But a few, like Jason Kidd of the 2011 World Champion Dallas Mavericks, will say things like "Stay focused." Prior to the Mavericks' final game against the Miami Heat in the 2011 NBA Finals, Kidd and Jason Terry were the only players who spoke—Kidd preached "focus" and Terry built up his teammates—but other than that the Mavericks' locker room, like those of most championship teams, was as quiet as a Sunday school class.

The fear athletes have is natural, and it can be used to advantage: fear keeps you on your toes and helps you focus your control. But sometimes there are situations beyond your control, and that is a different kind of fear. Experts call this "conditioned fear," which is different from the response to a lion attack or a mugger jumping out from behind a tree. Conditioned fear is learned and nurtured. It's the growing alarm parents feel when their daughter is late getting home from a high school dance, or the feeling you get when the doctor says you need "additional tests." It's the anxiety of waiting on mammogram results, or the back-of-your-mind dread that you'll suffer a heart attack, be diagnosed with cancer, or become paralyzed in a car crash. Some of these fears are rational (like poisonous snakes and high-crime neighborhoods), while others metastasize into phobias.

At the height of my career, I faced a frightening situation over which I had no control and I learned firsthand what conditioned fear feels like. My eyesight was deteriorating, and I had just been told that I would eventually go blind. First, I was scared. Then I became depressed, not gee-I'm-sad-my-team-lost depressed, but seriously, clinically, can't-get-out-of-bed depressed. No amount of training or experience can prepare you for the full range of emotions that you go through and the physical and psychological changes that manifest when you know that your world will grow darker by the day.

There were also a couple of other problems. First, I was a bobsled driver, the person responsible for piloting a projectile down the world's most treacherous runs—yet I had eyesight so bad I would have been kept from getting a driver's license in any state. That in and of itself should have caused a great deal of concern, and probably would have were it not for one very important detail, a detail that was perhaps even more problematic than the fact that I was going blind: I kept my condition a secret.

Nobody knew—not my teammates, my coach, or even my closest friends. Anyone with 20/200 vision is considered legally blind. My vision was 20/600 and getting worse by the day. Without the strongest contacts made, I couldn't see to get from the locker room to the starting line, and yet I kept it from everyone, even the three teammates who were putting their lives in my hands every time they jumped into the sled behind me.

It sounds crazy now. How could I have kept secret the fact that I was going blind? If I had been diagnosed with multiple sclerosis, cystic fibrosis, or some other terrible disease, keeping it from those around me would have been tough but manageable, at least for a while. But when someone you work with on a regular basis cannot see, you usually notice, especially after he bumps into a few things. Somehow I was able to keep everyone around me fooled, in part by insulating myself when I was away from the track and by remaining all business when I was on it.

Driving a bobsled requires explosive speed and strength, as well as quick fast-twitch reflexes. What it does not require is 20/20 vision. To understand how I was able to drive the world's fastest bobsled when I couldn't read a street sign on the highway, you have to imagine yourself sliding down a track with walls of ice on both sides and white turns straight ahead. Unlike race car drivers, bobsled drivers can't see much with all the curves, just the occasional visual cue like a flagpole or the passing edge of a grandstand. Daytona 500 winner Geoff Bodine learned this after he crashed and bent the frame during his first and only run driving a bobsled. We're actually a lot closer to air-show pilots, who see nothing but sky and ground when making their turns. Even before keratoconus started affecting my vision, I could see only a few feet in front of the sled during a run. I relied on my other senses, primarily feel, as gravity and speed pulled us into and out of turns. As my vision grew worse, that sense of feel more than compensated for my visual impairment.

This was not an excuse, or even a valid reason for keeping my condition a secret. Just as I didn't lose my sight in a day and didn't fall into the depths of depression in a week, my decision to keep my impending blindness from everyone came as gradually as a changing tide. Then my sight got worse. I kept telling myself that the answer was out there somewhere; I just had to find it. But with each new opinion, the prognosis grew worse. Still I didn't tell anyone. I hadn't said anything before, so it was easy not to say anything now. The longer I held my secret, the harder it became to confess, even as my condition worsened by the day.

The second problem was that I had finally started winning. After years of work, I was finally experiencing the kind of success that I'd been killing myself trying to achieve. So somewhere inside me, I hoped things would work out and I would never have to tell anyone that I had a problem.

Unfortunately, as the spotlight grew brighter, my ability to see it got worse, my depression deepened, and the pressure of keeping my secret intensified. By all rights my career was over, and I knew it. Everything I had worked for, everything I had wrapped my identity around, was fading like a movie screen going to black. Not only would I not reach my goals, but I would live my life either as a blind man or a transplant recipient, or so I thought. I had become a lot quieter as my eyesight worsened, which was not my natural personality. As a teenager I was the most outgoing person in my circle of friends—the life of the party, according to those who knew me best. But as my eyesight deteriorated, I found myself spending more time alone. When it came to the point that I had to take my contacts out and put on glasses, the guys on my team joked with me, calling me Mr. Magoo and saying, "Jeez, Holcomb, are you blind?" I didn't respond because the honest answer was, "As a matter of fact, yes, I am."

Finally, I had no choice—I had to tell my coach. Not only was it unfair for my team to continue working as hard as they were with the expectation of winning a World Championship or an Olympic gold medal, but I could no longer live with the knowledge that I might crash and injure—or kill—someone because I couldn't see.

Three months after the most successful American bob-sledding season to date in 2007, my team gathered in Calgary for the first of three one-week training sessions. Our coach, Brian Shimer, was, at that time, the most successful driver in U.S. bobsledding history. Now he was getting us ready to go further and accomplish more than he ever had. Calgary has one of the best push tracks in North America, an area where teams can simulate pushing and loading into the sled. A tenth of a second difference in start times—faster than most people can clap their hands—can translate into a three-tenths difference at the end of the run, which is an eternity in a sport like bobsledding. Brian wanted to make sure we stayed sharp and fast throughout the summer. The World Championship was coming up, and then the Olympic Games. Given the season we'd just had, this could be a historic time for USA bobsledding.

It was an extraordinary time, but my mind was elsewhere. I had just gotten the final prescription lenses, the strongest contacts made, and they weren't working. Every specialist I had seen had said the same thing: "You have to have a cornea transplant." None of them said, "You're out of the sport." But that was only because it was obvious. The procedure would involve having the front of my eyes lopped off and replaced with corneal tissue from a recently deceased organ donor. The recovery from that procedure is two years for each eye, which would take me out of the World Championship and Olympic Games and effectively end my career, even if there were no complications. Like organ transplant patients, cornea recipients are on anti-rejection drugs for the rest of their lives. I would also have to take a lot of precautions, and bobsledding wasn't one of them. One good thud during a run and my corneas could fly right out of my head.

It was over. Now I had to tell my team. First, my coach.

Before I even spoke, Brian knew something was wrong. I was rooming alone in the basement of the house we had rented, and I hadn't come out for two days. He had no idea how far I had fallen in my mind, or how the onslaught of the depression had become a familiar old friend that I simultaneously dreaded and welcomed. While my teammates were warming up for their workouts, I was in the basement. When I did come out, I was lethargic and unresponsive, a man with a thousand-pound weight on my chest and nowhere left to turn. Finally, Brian pulled me aside and said, "Holcomb, what's going on? Do you not want to be here? These guys are here to work and you're mailing it in. They're here for you. You need to show them that you care."

I wasn't in the mood for a lecture, so I turned away from him and said, "I've got bigger fish to fry right now."

"Bigger fish to fry!" he shouted. "What could be bigger than being an Olympic champion?"

There was no better time to tell him. The question had been asked. All I had to do was answer.

"Shimer, I have to retire."

"Retire! What are you talking about? You're twenty-seven years old. You just had the best year of your career. You can't retire. We're on the cusp of history here."

My lip quivered and my voice caught in my throat. I had to take some deep breaths. After a couple of seconds, I steadied myself. And then I said it.

"I'm blind."

TWO The Right Place

For the last fifty years, most top skeleton, luge, and bobsled athletes have come out of Germany and Switzerland, not because of some Germanic sliding predilection, but because those are the sports that kids watch and admire growing up. Place matters.

You have a better chance of being a world-class marathon runner if you were born in Nairobi than if you are a native of Copenhagen or Zurich. If you're a good athlete growing up in Puerto Rico, you're probably going to gravitate toward baseball as opposed to, say, figure skating, and a big kid from Tuscaloosa, Alabama, is much more likely to play football than hockey, just as a young person from inner-city Detroit is more likely to play basketball than cricket or golf.

A middle-class kid growing up in Sydney, Australia, is a lot more likely to swim than become a ski jumper, not because of his personal desires or innate athleticism but because of his environment. And you're a lot more likely to be a great golfer or surfer if you grew up in Florida or Southern California than in Manitoba, Canada. That is not to say that Californians are genetically predisposed to golf or surfing, just as it's wrong to assume that Kenyans are born with a long-distance-running gene. But if you assume that a certain percentage of any population will gravitate toward sports, it makes sense that the region in which a person lives will have some bearing on what sports they play. Those from the southeastern United States see football as the quickest path to praise and fame, while Minnesota kids learn to lace up ice skates and slap a hockey puck around before they can write their names. I come from the American West, where we have a lot of options: skiing, biking, and skating, along with the traditional American sports like football, baseball, and, to a lesser extent, lacrosse. You can also find a fair number of rodeo cowboys—ropers and rough-stock riders—athletes who might as well be Martians to people in New York but who actually attend colleges like Utah Valley University, Odessa College, and College of Southern Idaho on bull-riding scholarships.

My father was a carpenter in Park City, Utah, so our family skied. I had a pair of skis strapped on me by the time I was two. My sisters and I were always on the slopes by Thanksgiving, if not before. Tommy Moe was as big a star to my high school peers as John Elway, so it was natural for kids in our area to dream about being Olympic downhill ski champions. If Dad had worked in Sacramento, California, or Fort Worth, Texas, I probably would have focused on some other sport, but because of an accident of location, I was as at home on the ski slopes as Michael Phelps is in the pool or Kobe Bryant is on the basketball court. We were slide-down-the-mountain people, which set the direction of my life.

If I had any instinct that was not a result of my environment, I would have to say it was my natural attraction to extreme adventure. The winter before my fourth birthday, my parents put me on the slopes near our home and I took off with reckless abandon, forgoing the smooth snow of the trails and weaving through the trees as soon as I learned how to stand up and turn. One of the coffee bars on the runs at Park City was called the Snow Hut, which I loved as a small kid because of the smells and bustling, joyous activity that always seemed to emanate from its tables, inside and out. To get there, you had to ski down a relatively short but very steep hill. During one of my first runs, I skied away from my mom as fast as I could and headed for the hut. At the steepest part of the slope, I got into a full tuck—no poles—and shot straight down the fall line. I must have been quite a sight since I received a rousing cheer from all the adults.

I was competitive with my two older sisters, who were also athletes. Stephanie, twelve years older than me, played soccer and tennis and was on the gymnastics team throughout high school, while my sister Megan, eight years my senior, cross-country skied well enough to make the Junior Olympic team several times. Whether it was with a ball or on a bike, on skis in the winter or hiking the trails around the beautiful hills and streams of the Wasatch Range in the summer, I was always pushing myself, trying new things and doing whatever I had to do to not fall behind my sisters and their friends. A casual bike ride was a race in my eyes. Playing around in the backyard with a soccer ball became a contest. If one of my sisters did a flip on the trampoline, I had to match it.

Of course, being active had a price. At age five, I broke my arm from being bounced off a trampoline. That was the second broken bone I'd suffered in my relatively short life, the first coming when I was only six months old and I fractured a femur falling as I tried to pull myself onto a piece of furniture. And while I don't remember being in a tiny body cast as a baby, I do remember having my arm out of commission for six weeks from that trampoline disaster—an eternity for a rambunctious boy. So I made matters worse. The day I got the cast off my arm, I climbed onto a retaining wall to slide down onto one of the sturdy mailboxes that lined the streets near our home. I slipped and broke the same arm in a different place. Doctors were worried about all the broken bones, so they gave me a complete workup and interviewed my family members. It was determined quickly that I was a normal kid with a propensity to experiment—a trait I cultivated as I grew older.

—◦—

By the time I was eight years old, my mother, who did not share my penchant for adventure, realized she was going to hurt herself if she tried to keep up with me. So in 1987 my parents enrolled me in the "Learn to Race" program in Park City, a competitive ski school for junior Olympians, much like the Nick Bollettieri Tennis Academy in Bradenton, Florida, for rising tennis stars. Mom and Dad didn't know I was going to be an Olympian. No one in my family pushed me in that direction. They just needed me in an environment where I could ski as fast as I wanted while being safe and supervised. Learn to Race provided that. The racing aspect of it was a bonus.

That first year in the program, I gave Mom a framed photo of me medaling in my first ski race as an eight-year-old. As all moms do, she went overboard in her praise, raising her arms and feigning surprise at the gift. Then she took out a Sharpie and said, "Steven, you have to sign it for me. Someday you're going to be an Olympic gold medalist, and I want to be the first person to have your autograph."

She wasn't prescient, and she certainly wasn't a stage mom. Neither of my parents told me what I was going to do with my life. They just wanted to encourage me to be the best I could be at everything I tried. I was very fortunate in that regard. As I got older, I watched many of the kids around me struggle to please a father or mother who wrapped their relationships around how the child performed in a ski race. It was sad and a little depressing, especially when I saw how hard those kids worked, not because they loved the sport but because they thought cutting another second off a run would make their parents love them. My sisters and I played sports because it kept us outdoors and out of trouble.

When I wasn't on a run, I was thinking about a run. The father of my friend Jason Cole owned a ski shop in town and made several buying trips a year to Germany. On one of those trips he came back with a present for me. It was a small plastic luge and an action figure, about the size of a G.I. Joe, dressed in a body suit and helmet. I was so thrilled that I went into our backyard and piled up a huge mound of snow. Then I carefully carved out a sliding track with a dozen turns— the snow equivalent of a Hot Wheels track. It took a couple of tries to get the track exactly how I wanted it: fast, but not so fast that my figure would fly out. He was plastic and couldn't steer, after all. Once the track was perfect, I spent countless nighttime hours in the backyard creating imaginary races. The crowd always roared as my figure crossed the finish line first, and he would always jump up with his arms raised in triumph. Because my parents both worked—sometimes late—we never had a set bedtime, so I would stay out back playing in the snow long after other kids my age were either tucked into bed or sitting stupefied in front of the television. I dreamed of me being a winner like the G.I. Joe guy. At that age, all you want to do is be the hero. And so those nights in the snow were hours when a young boy's dreams of glory could be crystallized and embedded into the psyche.

—◅○▻—

As I grew older, in addition to the ski school, I became very competitive in soccer and football. When I wasn't on the field, I was riding my bike or doing something with the Boy Scouts. My father was into motorcycles, but that never appealed to me. Every time he revved the engine of a bike I would cover my ears and get as far away as possible. He tried to get me to ride with him, but even as a kid I found motorcycles rough, loud, uncomfortable, and smelly. I would much rather ride a bicycle along the Glenwild Loop trail, stopping to stare at the sunset or, later, to watch the multitude of stars that dotted a clear Western sky.

My mother and I would ride bicycles up and down the hills and throughout the neighborhoods of Park City. Those were the times when we would talk about our days and what was on our minds. I used to scare her intentionally by weaving in and out of the mailboxes that, to avoid snowdrifts, overhung the street. I would talk and look away, seemingly paying no attention, only to swerve out of the way a millisecond before my head hit the box. Mom would gasp, and I would chuckle. It was a wonderful place to be alive.

Now that I have traveled the world, I realize how fortunate I was to grow up where I did, not just because Park City was a winter sports town, but because of all the outdoorsmen who influenced me in my formative years. My soccer coach Dave Walters mentored me like a second father, encouraging me to give it my best no matter what I was doing. Then there was Randy Holmes, my Scout master, who taught me the value of doing a job right down to the last detail whether it was tying a knot, building a campfire, or pitching a tent. Randy took our Scout troop camping in the Goblin Valley crater in southern Utah. We played hide-and-seek and ran races through some of the most spectacular rock formations on earth. We also went canoeing on the Escalante River, where we learned the value of teamwork while experiencing the beauty of our state.

When Dave and his wife, Sherry, were not teaching us the nuances of soccer, they were riding mountain bikes or hiking with the area kids, anything to stay outdoors and active. Dave was one of the first people to teach me that talent alone was never enough to achieve greatness. "Talent is like a beautiful race car," he said. "If you don't set it up and drive it right, you'll run it into a wall. But if you work hard, keep it clean, and practice the right moves, you'll win more races than you lose." I didn't get the message right away, but I loved the imagery: a race car and its driver speeding around a track, each lap faster than the last. He also talked about things like focus and "harnessing my energy," which were equally tough for a teenager to understand. But I eventually got it. Through men like Dave and Randy and, of course, my parents, I learned the value of accomplishment, whether it was scoring a soccer goal, earning a merit badge, or helping Dad hang Sheetrock or frame a wall.

Sometimes the lessons on focus took a backseat to the energy and exuberance of youth. During an eighth-grade soccer game, I charged in from the wing, took a pass, and kicked the ball at the exact moment the goalie dove for the block. My shin caught him in the head, breaking both my tibia and fibula, but I made the goal, which was all that mattered. As I was lying on the grass in pain, the coaches running onto the field to check on me, the only thing I remember saying was "Did it count?" It did. We won the game.

All young males bounce around in their own skins for a while, seeking the foundations of an identity and molding the clay that will eventually become an adult personality. I was no different. I dyed my hair white with blue tips at one point. (Because I'm almost completely bald now, that comes as a shock to people who didn't know me then.) And I was the life of every party I attended. Unlike a lot of my classmates, I wasn't at all bashful on the dance floor, which made me quite popular with the girls.

One girl in particular, a very good skier named Tristan Gale, earned a lot of my attention. I knew Tristan the way kids in a relatively small, friendly town all know each other: we hung out and played when we were young, and then flirted with the boundaries of puppy love as we grew. The nice thing about having a girlfriend like Tristan was the fact that we were good friends before we dated and remained good friends after we broke up. During the time we were an "item" we shared a free-spirit mentality and a competitive nature that drove both of us to become better skiers and tougher athletes. We would hold hands as we rode the lifts together, but as soon as we got to the top, Tristan would say something like, "Okay, Holky, last down buys lunch," and she would take off.

I pushed myself to beat Tristan, just as I had fought hard to keep up with my sisters when I was younger. She also helped develop my maturity as we muddled our way through behaving as a couple in social settings like the prom. Because of Tristan, I learned to compartmentalize racing from the rest of my life. It's not easy for an athlete to turn the killer instinct on and off. Some people never learn to do it, which is why you see so many athletes struggle off the field or have trouble developing meaningful relationships. Because Tristan and I were both fierce competitors, we learned that we could try to beat each other down the slopes, but we could also put it all behind us after the race was over. That was tough for both of us at times, but because we cared about each other, we fought the urge to let our competitiveness turn petty once the runs were complete.

It is wonderful to remember those times, especially the tender goofiness (I once dyed my hair to match a prom tuxedo), but I also look back on those segments of my life as stones in the fortress that would become my future. Each experience prepared me for the challenges and expectations I would face later in life. Whether it was competing for a spot on a team or learning to get along in new and very different environments, the time I spent with Tristan and my friends in Park City helped craft the foundation of my career.

◄○►

I thank God for my parents. They were very supportive, realizing early on that racing was my passion. When The Winter Sports School in Park City opened, I was sixteen, and Mom and Dad sacrificed the financial comforts of the public school system and enrolled me in the private school for winter sports athletes. There were only seventeen students in my class, and we all studied together in a small building next to the construction scaffolding for the Olympic Sports Complex Sliding Track, which was being built for the Salt Lake Games. We went to school from April through November, giving us the entire winter off to compete.

At first I wasn't sure I wanted this setup, but then I learned that Utah had a law requiring that public schools allow private school and homeschool kids to compete on their sports teams and attend extracurricular functions. So I could still play football and soccer and go to dances and other events at Park City High School while attending The Winter Sports School. That did it for me. I attended school all summer while other kids were out on break, but when snow was on the mountains, I was out of school and competing.

Sometimes we would be racing for four or five straight weeks, traveling and hanging out with each other. We became a very close-knit group. In midsummer we would always travel to ski camp in Mount Hood, Oregon, where there is natural snow nearly year-round that is skiable well into the summer. Ski camp was a two-week-long strength and conditioning session where we would hike up the slopes carrying our skis for runs on rutty, ice-packed, "chattery" snow. (During ski races, an advantage of going first is that as more skiers go down, the snow gets bumpy. These bumps cause your skis to chatter. So we call the snow pack chattery, or chattered up.) After a couple of hours hoofing it up the mountain and skiing down, we spent the rest of our days running and lifting weights. The incline sprints were the worst—fifty yards as fast as you could go up a twenty-five-degree incline. More than once I thought my heart was going to explode. But I kept telling myself, *At least you'll be in shape for football.*

I was a running back and loved it. But at the beginning of my senior season, my football coach benched me for the first couple of games despite the fact that I was the fastest back on the team. My mother, who worked in the school system, confronted him about it. He said, "Steven isn't playing because he wasn't at summer practice."

Mom said, "You know that he was at ski camp, right?"

The coach nodded and said, "Yeah, all those spoiled rich kids go to ski camp."

Mom was having none of it. She explained the ski camp regimen and told the coach that what I had endured there was a lot tougher than anything he could dish out during spring football. The coach apologized. I started the next game and ran for a seventy-seven-yard touchdown on the opening play from scrimmage. The following week, I ran the opening kickoff back for a touchdown. I started every game the rest of the year.

—◁○▷—

In 1993, my parents divorced. That was tough on all of us, but I took it especially hard since I was still living at home.

Mom and I moved into an apartment over a garage owned by a friend, the father of one of my ski teammates, Katie Shackelford. That made our home very popular with all the guys in The Winter Sports School, who came over, hoping to spend a few minutes with Katie and her friends. Even though Mom worked two additional jobs on top of teaching to make ends meet, she was always unpretentious and welcoming, which made a rental unit feel like home. Most of my Winter Sports School buddies lived in million-dollar homes, yet our little apartment was one of the most popular gathering spots in town for junior athletes.

It was in that above-the-garage apartment that my friends and I would talk about where we hoped to go and what we wanted to do with ourselves after graduation. Most of those discussions centered on skiing. But by my senior year, I had come to certain conclusions: I was a good enough skier to place in regional and even national races. But I was not good enough to make the Olympic team and not close to good enough to medal in the Olympic Games. I couldn't even beat one of my best friends, Bryon Friedman. Bryon won a lot when we were growing up and went on to ski for Dartmouth College and was on the U.S. National Team. I figured if I wasn't better than Bryon, I wasn't likely to beat the Austrian or Norwegian downhill champions.

Coming to that conclusion was not hard for me, which, in hindsight, was unusual for a seventeen-year-old boy. High school seniors, especially athletes, usually view themselves as being somewhere between invincible and bulletproof. I had a pretty high opinion of myself, but I was also a realist. I had been on a couple of Junior Olympic teams, so I had seen the caliber of the competition up close. Not only was I not that good, but I realized I probably never would be.

Looking back on it now, I believe the fact that my life was so well rounded helped me see reality earlier and more clearly than others. Even though I had been skiing since before I could read, and all my adolescent dreams had been about becoming an Olympic athlete, I wasn't someone whose entire identity was tied up in one sport. Yes, I was a skier, but I was also a football player. And I was an Eagle Scout. My Eagle Scout project had been to build signs for the Rails to Trails bike paths throughout Park City, so I had tangible accomplishments beyond the slopes, things I could see and touch. I fear that too many young athletes, regardless of their sport, don't have a well-rounded perspective on life. They see themselves as track stars, or football players, or golfers, or figure skaters, and not as people. Because I had done other things, it was easier for me to see that skiing was not going to be my path to the Olympic Games. That didn't make it any easier— I was overcome with sadness when I realized I wasn't good enough—but it did allow me to see the truth. That realization also helped make my transition into bobsledding a lot easier.

—◁○▷—

Very few talented skiers (in fact, almost none of them) become bobsledders. Again, I look at where I grew up as one of the influencing factors in my decision to forgo skiing for the sleds. Since I was fourteen years old, Park City has had one of the only bobsled, luge, and skeleton tracks in America. That state of Utah built a lot of Olympic infrastructure in the late eighties in hopes of getting the 1998 Games in Salt Lake City. Even though the city lost to Nagano, Japan, by four votes, construction of the sliding track continued right next to our school. So, unlike in Aspen, Colorado, or Jackson Hole, Wyoming, bobsledding was part of the culture of Park City. My high school, The Winter Sports School, was next to the sliding track. It was our landscape, no different than the Starbucks down the street or the chair lift in the center of town. And because the track was there, nobody thought twice about a pickup truck with a sled in the back on Main Street.

My dad, who built custom furniture for the million-dollar homes and businesses around Park City, often drafted me when he got behind on a project, so it wasn't unusual for me to ride home tired and dirty after hauling lumber and hammering nails all day. One night, as Dad and I were returning from a construction site, we stopped at a Chevron station for a fill-up, some Doritos, and a Big Gulp. Parked next to us was a Ford Super Duty with a two-man bobsled in the back.

"Look at that," Dad said.

I grunted acknowledgment. I'd seen plenty of bobsleds before, so it wasn't as though we'd stumbled onto a golden chalice. If we'd lived in Lake Tahoe or some other ski area, that would not have been the case. Seeing a bobsled would have been a big deal in those areas, something worthy of my attention. At home in Park City, it was just an ordinary sighting of the day.

Dad went inside to pay for the gas, and when he came out he struck up a conversation with the sled's owner, who turned out to be Bill Tavares, an Olympic luger and bobsledder. Still, this wasn't a "Eureka" moment. I didn't go home thinking, *I've seen the light now, and I want to be a bobsled driver.* But I did look at Bill's sled and think, *That is pretty cool.* It was another kernel in the growing store of circumstances that would lead to where I am today, one I surely would never have experienced had I not lived in Park City.

Not everything was an accident of geography or fate. Just as is the case everywhere, Park City was full of guys who were more interested in beer and girls than in working toward a goal. I was not among them. The Olympic Games had been my dream since I had first crouched into a full tuck and rocketed down the slopes to the Snow Hut for some warm cocoa. My problem wasn't desire or work ethic or smarts; I just wasn't fast enough. Thousands of kids aspire to ski in the Olympic Games. Hundreds of those win races at the junior level. Only a few actually make it. I was not one of those. I was good enough to be a good junior, but I couldn't make the Olympic Team as a skier.

As easy as it was for me to see, it was just as difficult to accept, at least initially. It was like the high school football star who realizes he isn't a Heisman Trophy–caliber college player, or the kid who has wrapped his whole life into basketball, only to fail to make it at the next level. The Olympics was my Super Bowl dream, but once I graduated from high school, not nearly good enough at skiing, it appeared as though that dream was over. That was when I felt the first pangs of depression, like a yoke on my shoulders, pushing me down. There had to be another way. Surely this was not the end of the line.

Then, in the summer of 1998, an open call came out for the USA Bobsled combine in Salt Lake City. It was an open tryout for the bobsledding and skeleton teams, sports I had never tried and never even considered. I had seen plenty of bobsled runs—all you had to do was look up once the sliding track was complete—but I had never envisioned myself as one of the athletes. What had I to lose? Tristan and I decided to check it out.

The initial tryout consisted of six tests to measure general athleticism, specifically a combination of strength, speed, coordination, and explosiveness. The crowd of participants was bigger than I expected, and older. At eighteen, I was the youngest guy there by at least a couple of years. Some airmen came out from Hill Air Force Base, and there were football and track stars from the University of Utah. I didn't recognize anybody from the skiing community, but that was not a surprise. Skiing and bobsledding were as different as swimming and gymnastics. Thankfully, none of the guys I was competing against had any bobsledding experience either. Still, given the age gap, I wasn't sure how I would fare in a crowd of older, more seasoned athletes.

We were tested in thirty-, sixty-, and hundred-meter sprints. Then we had to make five large, continuous hops, and a vertical leap. Finally, we capped it off with a shot put test. It was sort of like the NFL Scouting Combine without the footballs. This was where I think being a multisport athlete helped me. I was accustomed to doing different drills for different sports, and my muscles and mind adapted quickly to these challenges. To my surprise, I was one of the fastest there, and I had the highest vertical leap in the group.

All the athletes were given points based on how they finished in each skill. You had to earn 675 points to advance. I made it on the number. At the end of the session, one of the coaches approached me and said, "Congratulations, Holcomb, you made the B team."

He said it with all the enthusiasm you might get from an auto mechanic congratulating you for not needing a new fuel pump. But I was overjoyed. In ski racing, the B team was one step below being in the Olympic Trials. You were one of the best in the world if you made the B team. What I later learned was that in bobsledding, there really wasn't a B team. You were either on a sled team or you weren't—B team meant I had advanced to the next stage of qualifying. I would get another shot, but there were no guarantees that I would end up anywhere but back home with Mom. At the moment, though, I was sky high and ready to slay the world.

"We would like for you to come to Lake Placid for the push championships in August," the coach told me.

With no job and nothing else to do in the late summer, I loaded up and headed east to New York for the quiet confines of Lake Placid. Even though Park City is not a big town by any means, it's a thriving metropolis compared to Lake Placid. Even as a naïve eighteen-year-old I remember thinking of this upstate New York town, *They held an Olympics here? How did anybody find this place?*

No matter. I had been given a second shot at my Olympic dream and I was not about to waste the opportunity. Lake Placid was a two-week training session, a tryout to learn how to push a two-hundred-pound sled from a standing start into something resembling a decent starting position.

Most athletes, no matter their conditioning, pull hamstrings or injure hips when they push a bobsled for the first time. That is one of the mechanisms the federation uses to whittle the hundred guys invited to Lake Placid down to thirty after the first week. If you pull a muscle or sprain a knee or ankle, you're out.

After the first cut, the training got even more intense as the team was pared down from thirty men to eight. Each run was timed. You were judged on how fast you got off the blocks, how fast you got to the sled, how quickly you pushed the sled a certain distance, and how many times you could continue that pace before falling out. It was a high-pressure test of physical and mental toughness, as well as strength and speed.

I had never pushed a bobsled prior to the Lake Placid session that September in 1998, but neither had any of the other invitees. Still, I felt like I had an advantage because I had been around bobsledding for years. I had seen practice runs and gotten to know guys like Bill Tavares, who would become an assistant coach for the USA Bobsled and Skeleton Federation. Watching doesn't replace training, but when everyone is a beginner, those who have at least been around a sport have an advantage, at least that is what I believed. And believing gave me a mental advantage over some of the guys in the group.

Once I made it into the top thirty, every hour became a pressure cooker. Every day I worried that I might screw something up. I was in fantastic shape, but as I watched one guy after another fall out—pulled muscle, sprained Achilles tendon, just not fast enough—I kept thinking, *I could be next. I have to give it everything this time out, because there might not be a next time.*

At the end of the week came a day that changed everything. I was told that I had made it into the top eight—that I was on the team, a part of U.S. bobsledding, but that because of my age and my size, the team would be taking the ninth-place finisher, a fellow named Doug Sharp, instead. It was at once the greatest and most depressing thing I'd ever heard. I had been good enough to make the team (and would, in fact, be listed on the U.S. bobsledding team roster)—through all the years of work and training and racing and preparing to be an Olympic skier, I never once thought I would be standing in Lake Placid at that moment, being told I was part of a team in a sport I had been involved in a grand total of three weeks. But I would be an alternate instead of a regular member of the squad, not because of performance but because of my age.

I thought I wouldn't be traveling, so I left Lake Placid and, like a lot of eighteen-year-olds, prepared for college. Because the training camp was in September, I'd missed the deadline for enrolling at the University of Utah, but never one to let such things stop me, I met with the dean and begged him to let me in. After listening to my pleas, the dean finally (and reluctantly) let me enroll. But the only classes available were upper-level courses, so I entered Physics 401, a senior-level class, as a freshman and began my career as a college student.

Six weeks later, I got a call from the folks at USA Bobsled. Because one of the eight qualifiers from the camp was injured, they needed me on the World Cup team. For the second time in two months, I sat down with the dean. Only this time, he wasn't so interested in my story. In fact, he didn't believe me. I begged him to give me incompletes instead of F's. Knowing that I had enrolled in upper-level classes, he thought this was an excuse to get out of flunking, so he said I'd need a letter from USA Bobsled confirming my story.

"You should already have it," I said. "I was told it would be faxed over immediately."

"Well, I don't," he said.

The meeting was over, and I was getting up to leave when his secretary stuck her head in the door and said, "I have something for you."

"Not now," the dean said, clearly annoyed at me.

Thank goodness for a persistent secretary who said, "No, I think you're going to want to see this," as she handed him the letter from USA Bobsled confirming my spot on the World Cup team.

I was given incompletes in all my classes at Utah, though the tuition was not refunded. At the time I didn't care (although my father was not at all pleased). Through luck, timing, and a confluence of forces I could never have dreamed possible, I was about to travel the world as a USA athlete.

It was the beginning of a journey I could never have imagined.

THREE
Right Time

When it came to being a bobsledder, my upbringing in Park City was a benefit, but timing also was critical. I was incredibly fortunate to try out at a time when American bobsledding was still small and hungry enough that a fresh, young upstart straight out of high school could make the team, and I had the good sense to be born at a time in which I could mature in the sport at the exact moment American bobsledding came of age.

It's a constant debate among sports fans: How would athletes from different generations fare in today's world? Would Cy Young win a Cy Young award if he pitched today? Would

Dick Butkus lead the NFL in tackles in the age of Ray Lewis? How many major golf championships would Ben Hogan win if he played against Tiger Woods and Phil Mickelson? They are unanswerable questions, and that's what makes the debate so much fun. But one thing I can say with certainty: if I had been driving the USA-1 bobsled in 1990, I would have had no chance of winning the World Championship, and the only way I would have won an Olympic medal is if thirty other teams came down with food poisoning. Timing matters.

—◁○▷—

Bobsledding did not originate as an American sport. Sleds have been around forever and have been referenced in writings as far back as 218 BC with Hannibal crossing the Alps, but the sport now known as bobsledding didn't come about until the late nineteenth century. The English take credit for it, claiming that a group of wealthy industrialists on vacation in Switzerland harnessed a couple of delivery sleds together, added a steering mechanism, and made merriment on the streets of St. Moritz. There is a good chance that this story is true, although none of the original Englishmen's names were recorded.

What is certainly true is that Caspar Badrutt, owner of the Krup Hotel in St. Moritz, and a master marketer, took the idea of steerable sleds through the streets of his town and came up with all sorts of variations—a two-man bobsled, a four-man bobsled, luge, and skeleton (when the driver goes down headfirst). The name bob-sled, or bob-sleigh, came about because of the way riders bobbed their heads back and forth on the straightaway as a means of propulsion.

Badrutt was soon marketing St. Moritz, already known throughout Europe as a mineral spa and getaway winter resort, where the well-heeled could frolic in the snow and enjoy new and exciting games involving sleds of all shapes and sizes. To further entice his guests (and squelch the complaints of the townspeople, who got right sick of drunk Englishmen clogging the streets and sliding headlong into their storefronts), Badrutt created a half-pipe sliding track. That was 1870, the year bobsledding officially became a sport.

Of course, it wasn't a sport like soccer or cricket or even golf; it was an amateur pastime for rich vacationers full of liquid bravery or foolish gusto. Teams were assembled pell-mell in the pubs or hotel smoking rooms, and each team member took turns driving until somebody got the hang of it. The tourists loved it. Before long, Badrutt was able to build the Palace Hotel near his track and market St. Moritz as a winter sports destination throughout Europe. Even vacationers from other Alpine countries took the train through the mountain passes to the tiny village 138 kilometers from Zurich.

It took fourteen more years to formalize the races. The first official bobsled race, where times were logged and prizes awarded, took place in 1884. The first club (the word the Europeans used before "federation") was formed in 1897. In the meantime, nationalistic pride caused athletes to begin to take the sport seriously. The Swiss couldn't very well have the

English beat them at an Alpine sport in their own country, and the English certainly didn't want to lose to the Germans. And nobody wanted to finish behind the French. So rather than throwing together a team of inebriated revelers, club members would draft athletes with great balance and hand-eye coordination. In some of the early bobsled photographs, it looks like sled owners went down to the loading docks and recruited the roughest and strongest men they could find for their teams.

By the early part of the twentieth century, the sport had branched out of St. Moritz and into parts of Germany, Italy, and France. Tracks were built solely for bobsledding, with each village and each country trying to outdo the other with the length, speed, and difficulty of its track. In 1923, the first international bobsled federation was formed just in time to add bobsled racing to the inaugural Olympic Winter Games in 1924 in Chamonix, France. The Swiss won the first gold medal, with Great Britain and Belgium taking silver and bronze. The sport was a rousing success and one of the most watched and enthusiastically supported events of those first Games. Everyone felt that bobsledding was here to stay.

The second Olympic Winter Games were held in St. Moritz, which was the logistical equivalent of holding the Super Bowl in Lubbock, Texas. It was a tiny town without ample hotel space, but the Games were not that big in those days. If a dozen people showed up for an event, it was deemed a success. Once again, bobsledding drew some of the biggest crowds, and the United States teams took gold and silver, one of only two times that has happened in the history of the sport (the other was the 1932 Olympic Winter Games in Lake Placid, New York).

As the sport evolved, the sleds became more complex. Rather than an elongated wooden toboggan with a couple of ropes tied to the front, bobsleds became metal structures with sides, and bobsledders became burly men who could weigh the sled down in the turns. And there were plenty of turns. Tracks became concrete covered in ice, usually 1,200 to 1,300 meters long with at least fifteen turns, one straight section, and a series of three quick turns in succession called a labyrinth. From there, designers got creative with the severity of the slopes and the angle and speed of the turns. Most tracks have a 180-degree turn with about 200 degrees of banking, meaning that it is literally possible to go through the turn upside down if you're carrying enough speed.

As tracks advanced, teams adapted. Soon there was an arms race between the teams, who wanted the fastest sleds, and event organizers, who wanted their tracks to present a fair and compelling test. Standards had to be implemented. So beginning in 1952, the international federation decided that four-man sleds could weigh only 630 kilograms (1,388.9 pounds) fully loaded, and two-man sleds could top out at 390 kilograms (859.8 pounds). Prior to that, some teams looked like they were on their way to a sumo wrestling match because a heavy team meant more downforce, which made the sled reach higher speeds while being easier to control. With the weight restrictions, as well as other standards—four-man sleds could not be longer than twelve and a half feet, for example—the sport was, technically, on more even footing.

But that's not really the case. After winning two of the first three Olympic gold medals in bobsledding, Americans quickly lost interest. For starters, other than Lake Placid, there wasn't a track in the United States, and the Olympic venue in New York might as well have been on the moon. Plus, Alpine activities were not high on the activity list for Americans during the Great Depression and World War II.

In the post-war era, skiing took off as America's winter activity. It was easier and, in many ways, more American: ruggedly individual and merit based—just you against the mountain. Sledding was what moms did in the driveway with their kids. Of course, U.S. bobsledding continued, and in fact Americans won the gold and bronze medals in the 1948 Games (again in St. Moritz) and silver in the 1952 Games in Oslo. But it is hard to judge the competition during those Olympics immediately following World War II because so many of Europe's great athletes were dead, and Germany was still in turmoil, being divided into two countries.

By the late fifties and sixties, the Alpine countries of Europe returned to prominence, with Switzerland capturing more Olympic medals, World Cup, and World and European Championships victories than any other country. Germany would hold that title if not for the fact that the country was divided into East and West Germany for forty years. East Germany rose to the pinnacle of the sport in the seventies because of the size and strength of its push athletes and the superior engineering of its sleds; after reunification in 1989, Germany became the dominant world force in bobsledding. Italy, Austria, and Canada had their moments as well. But from 1990 to 2005, the Germans and Swiss dominated the sport.

In the Winter Games, Americans preferred to focus on skiing, snowboarding, and figure skating—sports where there was a participatory tie-in with the fans. Kids in the United States might not be able to do a triple Salchow on the ice or a backside 520 on the half-pipe, but many of them had skated backward at the local rink or gotten a little air under a snowboard. Nobody in America grew up bobsledding, so the sport became like rugby, something cool to watch whenever it was on television, but not something fans were willing to follow or sponsors were keen on supporting.

As a result, American equipment became second-rate and our athletes, while good, were guys who had been snatched from other sports and trained to push and drive a sled.

That all began to change in 1992 because of the commitment of one man who loved his country and loved racing but who knew absolutely nothing about bobsledding. In a story that is stranger than fiction, a NASCAR driver became the sport's most unlikely hero, a man who stepped forward to rescue American bobsledding.

—◇—

The oldest of three stock car racing brothers, Geoff Bodine is listed among NASCAR's fifty greatest drivers. He grew up in

Chemung, New York, a tiny town in the western part of the state on the Pennsylvania state line, an area where boys in the fifties and sixties were expected to know how to tear down and bore out a car engine. Geoff's father and grandfather owned the town's racetrack, a three-eighth-mile oval called Chemung Speedrome. By 1954, at the age of five, Geoff was climbing behind the wheel of a micro-midget and hitting the track, which was dirt at the time. Saturday night racing was big business in rural America in those days, and the Bodines promoted races every week at the family's track. When they weren't selling tickets or racing themselves, the Bodine boys were entertaining themselves by pouring a bucket of car parts on the floor and seeing who could identify them all and explain what they did.

A gearhead who would race anything at any time, Geoff once dressed up as a girl when he was fifteen to get into a Powder Puff race. The family home was full of racing trophies before Geoff was old enough to drive a street car, and he quickly worked his way up through the various circuits. In his teens he made the jump to the NASCAR Modified Series, where the cars look like an amalgamation of hot rods and open-wheel Indy cars. It was in that series in 1978, at age nineteen, that Geoff set a Guinness World Record, winning fifty-five out of eight-four races, the most wins in a single season by any driver—ever. More than three decades later, the record still stood.

Once he moved up to the NASCAR Winston Cup Series (the top level of the sport, now called NASCAR Sprint Cup

Series), Geoff won the Rookie of the Year title in 1982. Two years later, he got his first win in Martinsville, Virginia. Two years after that, he won NASCAR's version of the Super Bowl, the Daytona 500. By the early nineties, already in his forties and recognized as one of the greatest race car drivers in history, Geoff had nestled into a comfortable routine. He raced in the Sprint Cup and Nationwide Series, racking up twenty-four career wins and 229 top-ten finishes. He had wealth and fame, a beautiful home in Concord, North Carolina, a thriving business, and a family who loved him.

The last thing he needed was a new project, especially in a sport he knew nothing about. But Geoff felt duty call, and he answered.

It started in 1992 during Speed Week in Daytona, seven days of racing festivities that begin with qualifying and end with the Daytona 500. In between, there are a couple of 125-mile races, a few concerts, practice laps, autograph sessions, and sponsor dinners, while fans have a rip-roaring good time up and down the beach. The Daytona Speedway is within walking distance of Ron Jon's Surf Shop, which sits steps away from the water. In fact, the very first Daytona 500 was held on the beach, a spot where the sand is so hard that rocket engineers used the miles of straight beach to set land speed records. Now the beach hosts one of the world's largest motorcycle ride-ins (Daytona Bike Week) and is home to the Ladies Professional Golf Association. But nothing compares to Speed Week and the 500.

Geoff was ready to race in 1992, but like most drivers, he

was spending his downtime during the week in a luxury motor coach that he had parked in the infield near the garages. The area is like a mini-campground for NASCAR drivers. During downtimes they retreat into their million-dollar homes-on-wheels for naps, a little television, and general unwinding before risking their lives at two hundred miles per hour.

The race is always in February, but in 1992 Speed Week happened to coincide with the Olympic Winter Games in Albertville, France. Everyone watched the Olympics, including the drivers. During one of his afternoon breaks, Geoff sat on one of the couches in his motorcoach and watched the Games. The event being aired was the two-man bobsled. A lot of people who normally wouldn't watch a bobsled run tuned in that year: Heisman Trophy winner and NFL running back Herschel Walker was making his Olympic debut pushing the two-man bobsled with driver Brian Shimer (who would later be my coach).

Brian was a flip-flops-and-sunglasses kid from Naples, Florida, who played running back and receiver for Morehead State University and had never seen a bobsled up close until 1985, his last year in school. "Heck, I'd never seen snow until I was in college," he said. Right after football season ended his senior year, he got a letter in the mail from the USA Bobsled and Skeleton Federation: a form note that went out around the country inviting athletes to give bobsledding a try. Brian had no illusions about playing in the NFL, and the prospect of being an Olympic athlete—being able to continue working out and competing and traveling the world—appealed to his

youthful sensibilities. He didn't have a job waiting after graduation and could see no downside in trying out, so he figured
he would give it a shot. "The danger sucked me in," is how
he described it. Just like me, he surprised himself by making
the team, especially since he was a warm-weather kid from
Florida. The very first bobsled race he ever saw was one that
he was in as the brakeman.

In 1988 Brian made it to his first Olympic Games in Calgary as the brakeman on the USA-2 four-man bobsled team.
"That was the year the Jamaicans had their first team, the
Cool Runnings year," he later said. "So, when people ask how I
ended up in the Winter Olympics, I always say the Jamaicans
came through South Florida on their way and picked me up."

Brian finished sixteenth that year, but the entire Olympic
experience had pulled him in. He wanted more, and he decided that to be the best he could be at the sport, he had to
move up front and become the driver.

By 1992, Brian was America's best bobsledding hope, although he was more known as the chauffeur at various times
for superstar athletes Herschel, NFL player Willie Gault, and
Summer Olympic hurdler Edwin Moses, all of whom wanted
to give bobsledding a try.

Geoff Bodine knew even less about bobsledding in 1992
than Brian did in 1985. But he knew Herschel Walker and
he knew racing. He understood what it felt like to pull hard
g's through a high-banked turn, and how critical it was to hit
the entry perfectly. He knew how dangerous it was to exit
one turn at full speed just in time to enter another one, and

he understood the focus it took to pilot a vehicle safely along the fastest possible line. The dynamics of racing a car were much different than driving a bobsled, but the physics didn't change.

Also like a lot of just-tuning-in Americans, Geoff wanted to see the U.S. team finish well. Brian was one of the best drivers in the world—certainly the best American driver we had—and Herschel was one of the country's most famous athletes. Everyone who knew anything about football had seen his strength, speed, and explosiveness. He was a world-class sprinter packed into 230 pounds of muscle.

They ran okay in their first run, but after the second run, it was obvious that Brian and Herschel, even with no flaws, were about seven-tenths of a second slower than the Swiss and Germans. Less than a full second seems like a miniscule amount to most people, but at the highest levels of Olympic competition, seven-tenths is an eternity. Once it became clear that Brian and Herschel would finish no better than seventh, and the Swiss and Germans would finish one, two, and three, with Austria and Italy right behind them, television commentator John Morgan told the audience why the Americans were struggling.

"One of the biggest challenges is the fact that the Americans have to buy their equipment from the Europeans," Morgan said. "There are no American-made bobsleds."

Geoff yelled, "What!" at the television.

Morgan went on to explain that since there were no American-made bobsleds, U.S. teams were at the mercy of whatever European manufacturer sold them their equipment. And a German supplier wasn't likely to give an American team the most cutting-edge stuff. That would be saved for the Germans. The same was true with the Swiss. The newest and best sleds would go to the home team; the leftovers were sold to the Americans.

Geoff was very familiar with that sort of arrangement. It happened all the time in NASCAR. If a non-big-time driver was able to cobble together enough sponsorship money for one or two races, he couldn't go out and build his own race cars. He'd go to somebody like Rick Hendrick or Jack Roush and either buy a car or buy an engine from one team, a body from another, and the rest of the parts from a third. But no matter how the deal was structured, the small-time operator was not going to show up on race day with the best equipment.

For a U.S. Olympic team to operate like a one- or two-race NASCAR team was, in Geoff's eyes, unacceptable. He would later learn that individual drivers bought and repaired their own bobsleds with no help from the USOC, a situation he called "unbelievable."

Throughout the rest of the 1992 Speed Week and after the Daytona 500, Geoff couldn't shake the thought that someone had to do something for our Olympic athletes. Having a U.S. team in a German sled was, well, un-American. So a couple of weeks after leaving Daytona, and after the closing ceremony of the Winter Games in Albertville, Geoff made a few phone calls and set up a meeting with USA Bobsled officials in Lake Placid.

The honchos of the bobsled federation were happy to meet with him and get a picture and an autograph or two, but they had seen a lot of people with a passing interest in the sport come and go. They didn't roll their eyes in front of him, but most of the officials were saying *Here we go again* to themselves when Geoff got there.

They did treat him to a thrill, though. Driver Bruce Rosselli said, "Geoff, do you want to ride in a bobsled?"

Of course he accepted. Race car drivers love speed. Geoff had flown with the U.S. Air Force Thunderbirds and raced some of the fastest cars in the world, so he couldn't wait to get in the back of a bobsled.

Bruce took off down the Lake Placid sliding track and scared Geoff half to death.

"Let's go again," Bruce said to a visibly shaken Geoff after the first run.

"No, I think I'm good," Geoff said. But Bruce insisted, and Geoff went for a second run.

The second time, though, he got the hang of it and wasn't quite as terrified. But then Bruce upped the ante again. "You want to drive it?" Bruce asked.

"Absolutely not," Geoff said.

Again, a lot of cajoling and needling ensued, until Bruce talked Geoff into the front of the sled. They didn't go from the top. Bruce found a spot where they could load about three-quarters of the way down the track. Not only would they not go quite as fast this way, but Geoff wouldn't have to maneuver through as many turns. It seemed like a great plan right up to the moment they got in the first turn. Geoff pulled the D-ring steering cable too hard and the sled started to nose down. Realizing that he'd oversteered, Geoff pulled the opposite ring to correct. But runners on ice are a lot different than wheels on asphalt. By the time Geoff made the correction, it was too late. The sled rode up the slope and slammed into the wall. Then it came out of the turn and hit the wall again, warping the frame. When they got to the bottom, the sled was totaled.

As Bruce stood dumbfounded, looking at his ruined sled, Geoff said, "Well, Bruce, I guess I'll have to build you a new one."

Nobody thought he was serious, but Geoff hadn't gone to Lake Placid for a photo op and a sled ride. He told the coaches and federation guys that he knew nothing about bobsledding but, he said, "I can promise you one thing: American Olympians will be in American-made sleds. You won't have to buy them. I'll provide them. And they'll be the best we can make."

The USA Bobsled folks were skeptical. This was not a sport you entered on a whim. A lot of guys in the past had gotten in with equally noble ambitions. They spent a lot of money before throwing up their hands and walking away. Everyone appreciated Geoff's enthusiasm and support, but nobody expected him to follow through.

What they didn't know was that this wasn't some hayseed grease monkey who tinkered with race cars. Geoff had been an innovator his whole life. He had brought power steering to NASCAR and was the first driver ever to use the full faceplate on his helmet to protect his eyes and cut down on glare.

When he returned to his NASCAR race shop, Geoff called a meeting with his chief engineer, his crew chief, his chief mechanic, his metal fabricator, and two of his partners and race car builders from Connecticut, Bobby Cuneo and Bob Vee of Chassis Dynamics.

"Boys," he said, "we're now in the bobsled business."

There was a long pause. Finally his fabricator said, "The what?"

When Geoff tells the story, he says he thought, *How hard could it be?* "We all thought we could build a good prototype for about $25,000."

He called another meeting with the USA Bobsled guys, this time in Connecticut at his shop. This time Brian Shimer attended. Geoff went through the same speech he'd made in Lake Placid, telling everyone that he was serious about building bobsleds in America—for Americans. Brian had heard it all before, and while he thought Geoff was a nice enough fellow, he didn't want a lot of people wasting their time. "Look," Brian said, "in my time in this sport, I've seen a lot of people come and go in terms of thinking they're going to build the next great thing. I know you guys are from NASCAR, but this isn't a car with wheels and an engine, and we don't run on a pavement. Bobsledding is like a controlled wreck. The only time you have control is in the curves. Other than that, you can't even point the thing where you want it. Gravity and ice is all you have."

Geoff was not deterred. He asked tons of questions. What did Brian mean by a "controlled wreck"? What made some sleds faster than others? How much drag did you experience if you did everything right in a turn? Far from being offended by Brian's comments, Geoff wanted to learn from them, to pick the brains of the driver to find out how to build a better machine. That was how things worked in NASCAR: the driver provided constant feedback. Sometimes it sounded like whining, and other times it sounded like two physicists talking about propulsion theory, but the give-and-take between driver and crew chief were a staple of all successful race teams.

Conversations like that never happened in bobsledding. Brian still wasn't totally convinced that this would go anywhere, but he walked out of that initial meeting thinking, *This guy might really be on to something.*

Geoff was committed to seeing the project through. He used a composite of his last name (Bodine) and his race car building company (Chassis Dynamics) to create a new venture called the Bo-Dyn Bobsled Project. Geoff put in the initial money. "It lasted about a month," he said. "I got a call saying, 'We need more.' So I sent more, and more, and more. I stopped counting after about $200,000."

What no one could have realized at the time was how much Geoff and his team's ignorance of the sport would turn out to be an asset. The engineers, fabricators, mechanics, and technicians took on the project without any preconceived ideas about sled design. They knew the dimensions and the weight requirements and they looked at other sleds, but that was it. The one thing they did know was racing. Whether it was trucks, cars, go-karts, or boats, Geoff's team knew how to make things go fast. With all the technology and testing they put into building a NASCAR race car, the Bo-Dyn guys set out to design and build American bobsleds.

It would be a great Disney-esque story if Geoff and his team came out of the shop on the first try with a super-sled that blew everybody away, but that is not how the real world works. Their first designs were okay, but they weren't faster than the sleds built by the Germans and Italians. Metallurgy and the laws of physics don't change from one sport to the next, so while Bo-Dyn caught up quickly, it couldn't out-engineer the Germans in a sport the Alpine countries had been working on for seventy years.

But what Geoff could bring was a different philosophy to the bobsled track, a philosophy of constant improvement, instant correction, and continuous communication. Prior to Geoff's entry into the sport, bobsled drivers were responsible for their own maintenance. Drivers like Bill Tavares and Brian Shimer would work on their sleds all summer, honing and tuning and getting them as ready as possible, but once they put them on the ice, if the sleds didn't work, that was it. Tough. They were stuck with what they had until the next season. The drivers also carried their own tools, usually in a single toolbox. If there were any major problems, the race was lost.

In NASCAR garages, if a car didn't work, you rebuilt it overnight. That was the mentality Geoff brought to the ice. When Bo-Dyn put its first sled on the ice in the 1993–1994 season, Geoff brought the NASCAR pit crew concept to bob-sledding. While other teams showed up with a driver, pusher, coach, and toolbox, the Americans were suddenly arriving with pit carts and a crew that could rebuild an entire sled overnight if necessary.

In the beginning the Europeans looked at the Bo-Dyn guys and said, "What do they think they're doing?" Every other team shipped its sleds to events in single crates, but the Bo-Dyn equipment came in two, sometimes three crates: one for the sled and the others for welders, tools, sheet metal, parts, toolboxes, computers, and anything else needed to dial in a sled on the spot. If the driver was having trouble turning the sled in the labyrinth, the crew could tweak the runners, adjust the ropes, and perhaps pitch the nose down in one direction or another to improve control. It might have looked like a joke to some of the other teams, but when the American teams started getting faster, and when the Germans and Swiss realized that our teams could change out cables and runners on the spot, they ramped up their own operations to keep up with this American bobsledding, NASCAR style.

"I can't tell you how many hours upon hours we spent in the garages changing things: cutting frames, changing runners, doing everything overnight and trying it out the next day," Brian said. "That's when I knew that this project was going to work. With Geoff, we were really on to something."

--◄o►--

Geoff never promised that his sleds would win medals, but his competitive nature kept pushing him to make Bo-Dyn better and better. In the 1998 Games in Nagano, Japan, USA-1 finished two-hundredths of a second off the medal stand. American bobsledding was on the cusp of breaking out in a very big way.

Six months after Nagano, I finished eighth in the U.S. National Push Championships at Lake Placid and eventually earned a spot that year on the USA Bobsled team, coming into the sport at the same moment that Geoff Bodine began making very fast sleds.

The timing could not have been more perfect.

If I had been ten years older, coming into the sport in 1988 instead of 1998, I would have struggled the way Americans had for two generations—buying equipment from Italy or Germany or France, grabbing a hammer and a wrench, and hoping for the best. But because my entry into the sport coincided with the rise of American bobsled design under the leadership of Geoff Bodine, I was able to compete at a level no American had in half a century.

FOUR

Push, Ride, Repeat

The only way to gain experience is through experience. It's such a corny cliché that everyone rolls their eyes when you say it, but practice really does make perfect, or close enough to perfect that the average person cannot pick up any imperfections. The greatest athletes make it look easy because they have practiced so long and hard that complicated and physically demanding actions like making a three-point jump shot off a fast break, kicking a fifty-yard field goal, or hitting a golf ball three hundred yards look effortless.

Great bobsledders are no different than basketball players, baseball pitchers, or classical musicians: they work their butts off to make it look easy, pushing the sled, getting into the sled, riding down the run, and then doing it again and again and again. Push, load, ride, repeat. There is no magic formula, no innate athletic gift that bobsledders possess. Yes, all world-class bobsled athletes are strong, fast, quick, and coordinated, but are we stronger and faster than the average NFL fullback? Are we quicker and more coordinated than a semifinalist at Wimbledon? Of course not. What makes those athletes great at their sports is what makes Olympic bobsledders great at ours: we practice.

Herschel Walker and Edwin Moses were fine pushers when they tried bobsledding, but neither of them left with a medal, just as I would not do so well at NFL training camp or in a USA Track & Field competition against Walker and Moses respectively. That is one of the reasons athletes enjoy watching other sports. Kobe Bryant spent a lot of time in the National Aquatics Center in Beijing watching Michael Phelps, not because they were close, personal friends but because Kobe appreciated the skill, effort, and dedication it took for Michael to become one of the most decorated swimmers in Olympic history.

Best-selling author Malcolm Gladwell puts the practice needed to reach "expert" levels at ten thousand hours. The example he used that I appreciated the most was The Beatles. Because I wasn't around during the John, Paul, George, and Ringo era (I was born the year John Lennon died), I had to rely on conventional sources to learn the history of the band. According to everything I'd ever seen, the band played together in the late fifties in Liverpool and burst onto the scene in the early sixties with a trip to America. Like a lot of people, I figured the band got lucky. The band's look and sound lined up perfectly with the fads of the day. But Gladwell proved that the conventional story was wrong. Not only had John and Paul been playing together for almost a decade when they finally hit it big, but the band perfected its sound in the strip clubs of Frankfurt, where it was the house band for every girl on the stage, sometimes playing ten or twelve hours a day. The Beatles practiced at least ten thousand hours in the German underground before the Fab Four ever put on skinny ties and combed their bangs down over their eyes.

I've never done the math, but Gladwell's ten-thousand-hour rule seems about right. Becoming an expert bobsledder, like anything else, requires a lot of time, focus, and repetition. In my case, I had to spend many hours on the ice and even more in the gym.

When I got the news that I had made the USA Bobsled team, I celebrated like any eighteen-year-old would. But since I'd been named an alternate due to my age, I was on my own for training. So I asked the inevitable question: What now? The answer was simple: I was headed home to Park City to start working as a push athlete for one of the team drivers, a fellow named Travis Bell, who lived about thirty miles away in Salt Lake City.

Travis was the perfect bobsled pilot to break in a rookie. Mild-mannered but knowledgeable, experienced, detail-oriented, and talkative, he was like a combination coach and teammate. He critiqued every run and walked me through how we could be better and faster. To the average person that sounds silly. How could someone coach you on pushing? You just run faster or push harder. But that would be like saying, "How could someone coach you on golf? You just hit the ball toward the hole." There are hundreds, perhaps thousands of ways to improve the speed and consistency of a bobsled push, just as there are myriad ways to improve your swing and stance in golf. Length of stride, leverage, weight distribution, foot position, traction, loading: these were all intricate, athletic skills that I had to hone. A runner might show up at track and field camp with a lot of natural speed, but coaches, trainers, kinesiologists, motion-efficiency engineers, along with countless hours of work, transform a talented runner into a world-class Olympic sprinter. The same is true for bobsledding. The tryouts in Salt Lake and Lake Placid identified my raw abilities, but only practice and coaching would mold me into an award-winning bobsledder.

If I had any advantage, it was the number of hours I had spent as a skier. Even though I'd never ridden in a bobsled, I understood the focus required to shave a tenth of a second off a long, fast run. I also understood that two-tenths of a second was the difference between finishing first and finishing off the medal stand. Minuscule amounts of time—faster than a couple of blinks of an eye—were the difference between being a champion and an also-ran. I knew that the slightest mistake, a tiny bobble, a half-a-misstep, could be disastrous, even though I didn't yet know what those mistakes looked and felt like during a bobsled run. My experience would have been like an American football player transitioning to rugby. The game is radically different, but the mentality it takes to run a ball across a goal line without being tackled is the same, even if every other aspect of the game requires learning new skills.

Every day I was on the track with Travis was like being in a one-on-one classroom. He answered every question I had, even when I was asking about things that had nothing to do with pushing the sled. We discussed every intricate detail of the sport.

I also had to grow accustomed to the feel of riding in a bobsled. Unlike other American sports, there was no peewee or Pop Warner bobsledding. Kids grew up sliding toboggans down driveways, but unless you lived in a snowdrift area of the country and had enough time and resources to carve your own track, there simply wasn't a spot to learn the sport of bobsledding until you were into the sport competitively. So I experienced my first sled rides like any rookie: with wonder and more than a little fear.

Roller coasters are often used as examples of what a bobsled run feels like—I've used that example many times—and in terms of the sensation of being propelled downhill at ninety miles an hour through hairpin turns and ninety-degree embankments, the scariest roller coaster you've ever ridden is as close an example as you can find. But roller coasters don't go continuously downhill, nor do they force you to pull as many g's as you do in a bobsled. The two most important differences are: a roller coaster is locked onto a track, whereas bobsleds, of course, are not—somebody has to drive the thing. And, second, you're harnessed into a roller coaster, while in a bobsled there are no padded roll bars or shoulder straps. Once you hop in, it's up to you to hang on throughout the run.

The turns are different as well. Unlike a curve on a road or even the turn you make through a gate on a ski slope, the banked turn has three distinct parts: the entry, the apex, and the exit. You enter a turn on a line so that you can hit the apex (the center of the turn, and sometimes a double apex—one curve in Altenberg, Germany, has four apexes) high enough so that gravity and momentum shoot you through the exit as fast as possible while setting you up for the next turn. It sounds simple enough, but when you hit your first turn in a bobsled, you realize that it is like nothing you've ever experienced. Stunt pilots don't pull as many g's, which means your skin and muscles feel like they are being vacuumed away from your skeleton, and the blood rushes from your head. Oddly enough, the apex of a turn doesn't pull you to one side or the other: it pulls you down. The embankments make the center of a turn feel like you're hitting a dip in the road at a very high speed, or like you're hitting an updraft in a plane. Your body tenses as you feel your internal organs shifting downward, and you instinctively flex the muscles in your neck to keep blood from fleeing your brain.

In those first days, I also learned the value of trust on a bobsled team. Travis trusted me to get us off to a good start, and once we loaded, I trusted him to pilot the sled quickly and safely to the bottom. That was tough, initially. Even though I had been on teams my entire life, I had never entrusted my life to anyone on my soccer or football teams. The closest I'd come to that kind of total trust and commitment was in the Boy Scouts when we would climb rocks or canoe through rapids. Those were dangerous situations where you could get hurt if you or your teammate screwed up, but they were nothing like what could happen in the middle of a bobsled run.

Ski racing was just as dangerous. Catch an edge, get out of position, take one wrong line, and you could be seriously injured or killed no matter how experienced you were. But a skier is the master of his own fate. He doesn't have to trust anyone else to drive him through a run. It's just him against the mountain. That was not the case in bobsledding. The push athlete had to trust his driver, not only to make a fast and flawless run but to get everybody down in one piece.

While it never showed in my performance as a push athlete, I never fully let go of my need to be in control. That was why I would eventually become a driver. But in the beginning, as I was learning how to push and load and ride, I found myself saying a silent prayer before every run: *Lord, don't let me screw up this start, but for goodness sake don't let Travis screw up on our way down.*

The final thing I found surprising during those early runs was just how blind a bobsled run was. During most roller coaster rides, you can at least see where you're going. Once you load into a bobsled, the thing you see is ice and the occasional flash of sky. A flagpole or a grandstand might whiz past every now and then, but for the most part, drivers and pushers see almost nothing but white walls and the sheet of ice beneath us. We are like stunt pilots flying through the clouds with one very important exception: stunt pilots have instruments in the cockpit to tell them where they are.

Travis and I worked hard, and I soaked up as much as I could during our time together. I had no idea how long he and I would work together before either of us got into a race, so I looked at every run as a challenge and an opportunity. I wanted each second on the track to be productive and I wanted each run to be better than the last.

It's difficult now to look back on that time and know how good or bad I was because I had no frame of reference at the time and everyone assumes he is better than he really is during the heat of the moment. If I had a chance now to see those first runs on tape, I'm sure I would shake my head. There is no way, given where the sport is today, that I would hire the eighteen-year-old version of myself as a pusher for USA-1. So I was once again a fortunate recipient of timing and circumstance when I got a call from one of the team coaches a month into my training with Travis. One of the pushers on USA-1 had been injured. I was needed in Calgary—immediately.

It was time to race.

—◦—

The Olympic Games had been in Nagano, Japan, the winter before, and as usual, the Germans and Swiss dominated in the four-man competition. Nagano produced a couple of unusual results. In the four-man race, Great Britain and France tied for third with times of 2:40.06. Since Olympic races are timed to the hundredth of a second, the two teams shared the bronze medal. Even stranger, in the two-man race, Italy and Canada also tied with times of 3:37.24, only that draw was for first. Pierre Lueders and Dave MacEachern of Canada and Günther Huber and Antonio Tartaglia all crowded onto the gold medal podium and listened to two national anthems.

The United States didn't scratch in either race. Driver Jim Herberich and his pusher, Robert Olesen, finished seventh in the two-man race, a full 1.3 seconds off the pace, while Brian Shimer and his crew of push athletes, including Chip Minton, Randy Jones, and Garrett Hines, finished fifth, just two-hundredths of a second away from making it a three-way tie for the bronze.

Coming off an Olympic year, there were lots of shakeups in the teams. Unlike baseball or football or any other professional sport where, if you don't win the Super Bowl or the World Series, you always have next year, Olympic athletes have very few opportunities to realize their dreams. Robert Olesen, for example, went back to track and field, which was his background. He would later become the track and field coach at the University of North Carolina at Charlotte. But that sort of career path was not unusual. If a sprinter or skier or bobsledder stays in the sport a dozen years—which is a very long tenure for a high-level athlete—there will be only three Olympic Games in that time frame. That's three opportunities in a lifetime to not only qualify for the Games but compete and, hopefully, medal. After Nagano, some guys would call it a career, while others would try to hang on until the 2002 Games.

Most Americans wanted desperately to make the 2002 Games, given that they would be held in Salt Lake City. Everyone wants to be a part of the Olympics in their home country. But with the hangover from Nagano still fresh, the Salt Lake City Games seemed an eternity away. In the fall of 1998, most teams just wanted to get through the World Cup season with some decent showings, maybe a win or a medal or two. This was reevaluation time, an opportunity to test new equipment and put new talent to the test.

I was one of the fresh bodies who got run through the wringer. Our first event was in Calgary, Canada, which wasn't much of a culture shock. Going to Alberta was like going to Montana. They had cowboys and ski bums, hot coffee, and cold beer, just like we had in the United States. The biggest blow was seeing how good the competition was. Being a rookie I had no idea what to expect, but what I learned very quickly was that bobsledding was a dog-eat-dog world like everything else. The German team wanted to cut our hearts out in the off-year race in Calgary just as much as it did in the Olympics. And if having to face down the best bobsledders in the world weren't enough, you always had to look over your shoulder at your own team to make sure somebody wasn't jockeying for your job.

Because experience is critical, and the only way to get experience is to be on a team and in competition, I was very fortunate to find my way onto that 1998 World Cup team. What I didn't realize was that the culture shock had yet to begin. We went from Calgary back to Park City for the second event of the season, where we finished sixth. Two weeks in and I thought I'd gotten the hang of it. Then we packed our bags and headed to Altenberg, Germany, the most feared track in the world.

Injuries were common at the Altenberg track. That would continue to be the case for many years. As late as 2012, the Canada-2 four-man sled crashed, sending three of the four team members to the hospital.

But the difficulty and danger of the track was only a fraction of what I had to overcome. As an eighteen-year-old, the only foreign country I'd ever visited was Canada, which was a lot more like home than a lot of places in the United States. As a Junior Olympic skier, my travel had been limited to the United States and the provinces of Alberta and British Columbia. I'd never even been to Quebec, so English and the occasional "eh" was the only language I'd ever heard on the road. That changed in a matter of seconds when we got to Germany.

I couldn't say "hello" in German: *Hallo*. And unlike cities such as Zurich and Geneva where almost everyone spoke a little English, places like Altenberg, Germany, and Cortina d'Ampezzo, Italy, were relatively isolated Alpine villages where you could go days without hearing an English word and where you could spend your whole life without seeing a taco or french fry. I had to use sign language to order lunch and struggled to pay for it after I did. I couldn't read the signs, couldn't ask directions, and couldn't even plug in my CD player because I didn't know enough to bring a European adapter. I had also never experienced jet lag, which made me a lot of fun to be around the first couple of weeks we were in Europe.

From Germany it was off to Switzerland and then Italy, then back to Germany, and then Switzerland again, and finally to France. My stomach rebelled at least a dozen times in that first year, and I embarrassed myself more times than I care to remember. Thankfully, bobsledding was not on most people's radar, so I was able to perform like a rookie outside the spotlight and without a lot of grand expectations.

We did fine, but came nowhere close to winning a title. As a result, I was able to spend a lot of time in the sled, gaining experience with each run and putting in the practice needed to mark my spot on future teams. It was training I could not have gained any other way. And I am fortunate and eternally grateful to have been given that chance.

FIVE
Army Strong

Olympic athletes don't get paid for being Olympians. If you're in professional sports like basketball, tennis, or hockey, or if you can fill arenas by putting on shows like figure skaters do, then you're probably not worried about where the next paycheck is going to come from. Also, if you are successful in a sport where companies line up to pay for endorsements—track and field (Nike, Adidas, Reebok), swimming (Speedo), downhill skiing (K2, Salomon, Rossignol)—then you at least have an avenue to make a living. Michael Phelps has no trouble paying his light bill, not because Olympic swimming pays well but because he is a very successful spokesman for companies of all shapes and sizes. Apolo Anton Ohno also has a steady income stream from endorsement and appearance fees, as do Shaun White and Lindsey Vonn, which is great because short-track speed skaters, half-pipe snowboarders, and downhill ski racers make decent but not exorbitant prize money in their sports.

There are a lot of factors that go into making an athlete marketable. First you have to be recognized. Aaron Rodgers was the best quarterback in the NFL and a Super Bowl MVP when State Farm poked fun at his anonymity in an advertisement—"Oh, you're a dancer?" "No, I'm a quarterback." But Rodgers is not alone. A lot of football players walk around relatively unknown, in part because football is a team sport but also because they wear helmets. Take Maurice Jones-Drew or Ray Rice out of uniform and most people would pass them a hundred times without a second look. Quarterbacks have an advantage because they are the faces of their teams, but how many people could pick Matt Ryan or Joe Flacco out of a lineup? And the NFL is the most popular and profitable sporting league in the world. But when you get down to sports that people watch once every two to four years, the athlete Q scores tumble.

Bobsledders have everything working against them. We are not paid professionals; we are in a sport that most casual observers follow only during Olympic years; we wear helmets that hide our faces; we climb into sleds that hide our bodies; and we have no natural corporate tie-ins. Casual weekend winter-sports enthusiasts don't bobsled. Olympic skiers can at least promote skis, boots, apparel, etc., and snowboarders can endorse a myriad of products that go along with the shredder lifestyle. Bobsledders have nothing. Our sport is more like fencing—fun to watch but difficult to market. That presents a challenge when it comes to making a living. It's hard for bobsledders to pay the bills and eat while training and competing.

I was only nineteen as I entered my second season, so I didn't have a lot of expenses, but I still had to eat and drive and liked to go to a movie once in a while. Plus, I was traveling all over the world. There is no lonelier feeling than being hungry and broke in Munich, where few speak your language and cheap hamburgers are impossible to find. The stipend paid by the USA Bobsled and Skeleton Federation was just enough to keep me from starving to death. Beyond that, I had no income and no prospects. To advance in the sport, I had to continue to be on the ice from the fall through the spring and in the gym all summer, so a traditional job was out of the question.

If I took time off to earn some money, my spot would be filled by the next person in line. Experience is very important in bobsledding, so those with a season or two under their belts always have a leg up on newcomers. And competition remains fierce. If I had lost focus or gotten out of the sport for a while to earn some money, there is a good chance I would have been out for good. The next strong, fast rookie would have jumped in and taken over.

In my second season, I pushed for Todd Hays, the driver for USA-2. Our two best drivers at the time were Todd and Brian Shimer, with each battling for the top spot. I was lucky to have good working relationships with both. Much of our time was spent on buses and trains, in houses or hotels. That gave us a lot of time to talk and bond and work through any problems. I did everything I could to soak up information from Todd and Brian. None of us went out much. Even the established guys who had been in the sport for years weren't well-heeled enough to party in St. Moritz, where a glass of orange juice can run you five dollars. So we spent a lot of time together watching FIFA soccer matches and playing video games (I became the resident expert at both, having played soccer and knowing Super Mario Bros. inside and out).

After six months in Europe, where we finished tenth in the World Cup standings, our team returned to the United States and entered the U.S. National Bobsled Championships, a small event with a grand name. Unlike skiing or skating or track and field, the U.S. Nationals in our sport had only three or four sleds entered. Every American bobsled team was already committed to a World Cup schedule, so unlike skiing and skating where the championships are a huge deal, most of our guys greeted it with a smile and a shrug.

Our team won the U.S. National Bobsled title with Todd driving. All victories are nice, but this one didn't grab a lot of headlines. At the time, I celebrated it as a decent addition to my résumé, understanding that people within the sport knew where it fell on the priority list.

But I have learned through experience that you should never underestimate the importance of the seemingly mundane events in life. You never know who is watching. There are occasions where things that don't appear important at the time turn out to be the ones that change everything. This was one of those times. Not long after winning the national title, women's assistant bobsledding coach Bill Tavares (the man whose sled I saw in Park City all those years before) approached me about the Army World Class Athlete Program. Bill was a soldier in the program and loved it.

"It helps Olympic athletes train for their sports while also being in the Army," he said. "You join either the regular Army or the National Guard, [then you] go through basic training, and become an active-duty soldier—but your orders are to train for your sport."

At the time the program was headquartered at the Pentagon. The Army would later move the base of operations to Fort Carson, Colorado, which made sense for Olympians. The United States Olympic Committee is headquartered in Colorado Springs, Colorado, and many of the athletes live on campus when they aren't on the road.

When Bill approached me, it was pre-9/11, so nobody was thinking about war. The idea of serving my country as a member of the Utah National Guard and earning a paycheck while training for bobsledding seemed almost too good to be true.

"Why would the Army do this?" I asked, certain that there had to be a catch.

"Recruitment," Bill said. "You'd be a soldier first, but as a world-class athlete you would also be one of the Army's best recruiting tools. Athletes from the program attended over fifty recruiting events last year. The results were very good."

That made sense. I did a little more research and saw that the Army WCAP was perfect for what I needed. I signed up and became a member of the Utah National Guard.

Even though my orders through WCAP were to train and compete, I had to choose an Army specialty, so I chose the Engineering branch, one of a host of fields available. Now that we have come off a decade of war, most people imagine the Army as men with guns engaging the enemy. And that is one branch: Infantry. The Infantry soldier (and the Rangers and Airborne, which are elite groups inside the Infantry) are the boots on the ground, or "the tip of the spear," as the Army calls it. But there are plenty of other branches. The guys in tanks are in the Armor branch, while those flying helicopters have branched Aviation. There is Artillery and Signal Corps, Special Forces and Psychological Operations. There is even a dental and veterinary medicine branch, because soldiers need dentists and their animals need vets. My branch, Engineering, encompasses the soldiers who build bridges and roads and airstrips during combat, and who destroy the bridges, roads, and airstrips of the enemy. My military occupational specialty (MOS) was Combat Engineer, one of the most dangerous jobs in the world.

Need a bridge blown up before the enemy can cross it? Combat engineers are the guys you call. Not only do the engineers understand explosives, but they know where to put the charges so the bridge or tower comes down with one blast. That was my specialty: demolition. If a convoy on maneuver ran up on a boulder or a couple of trucks or a pile of debris in the road, my job was to destroy the obstacle and clear the path. And while that sounds cool—especially the part where you blow stuff up—during combat there is usually a reason a boulder or a truck or a cluster of junk is in the road, and it isn't by accident. For centuries combatants have put obstacles in the path of the enemy and lain in wait to ambush them when they stop to clear the way. That means the guys who clear the obstacles—in the case of the U.S. Army, the combat engineers—are the first targets for snipers, land mines, or improvised explosive devices (IEDs). One of our officers told us that the typical combat engineer commander expects a fifty percent casualty rate during combat operations, and the average lifespan of a combat engineer in a firefight is six seconds. Those guys are the first to go when the shooting starts.

Even with those dire statistics in mind, training was a lot of fun. In addition to learning basic soldier skills like saluting, marching, and shooting, I learned the proper way to detonate a land mine and how to blow up a roadblock. I also ran and did push-ups and sit-ups. Being a seasoned athlete, I was in the top of my class in the physical fitness test at both basic training and advanced individual training.

I was also trained to remain calm and logical under stress. Whether it is a drill instructor screaming at you to keep your weapon dry as you crawl through a mud puddle under barbed wire, or carefully arming explosives with gunfire going off all around you, the Army prepares you for the unexpected. You learn how to lead men, how to follow orders, and how to finish a job no matter what. The mission must be completed.

In training, I blew up a bus. We were simulating troop movements through an urban environment, having no idea that three years later American forces would be fighting house to house through the streets of Iraq. A platoon in three Humvees with one M1 Abrams tank had to stop progress because of a bus in its path. After guys with guns secured a perimeter, an explosive ordinance device (EOD) technician decked out in a bomb suit that looked like what the Apollo astronauts wore on the moon walked ahead with a grapple hook. He threw the hook every few feet and dragged it back to make sure there were no land mines in the path—a low-tech and dangerous way to find out where death lurked, but it was also effective, as humans were a lot more relentless in their search for mines than robots.

Once it was determined that there were no mines in our path, I came forward with my training kit, which included M1 dynamite, M1A4 priming adapters, shock-tube detonators, and blasting caps. I determined the quickest and most efficient way to destroy the obstacle and placed the explosives in exactly the right spot for maximum effect. Not only did I have to move carefully with all those explosives but I had to do so quickly. Every second that the men in the convoy were stationary, they were targets. So was I, but my responsibility was to clear the path and get the platoon rolling. After setting the charges, the EOD technician and I beat feet away from the scene, careful to travel only on the path we'd already checked for mines.

We knew this was a drill. There were no land mines in Utah, but the purpose of training was to simulate combat as closely as possible. If we'd ventured outside the area the EOD tech had already cleared, we would have possibly been called dead, and that would have led to what the Army liked to call "correction," some disciplinary measures that would have been very unpleasant.

We stayed on course and detonated the explosives, blowing the bus to bits in spectacular fashion. The convoy progressed without incident.

A lot of people have poked fun at the National Guard over the years with such terms as "weekend warriors" and "toy soldiers," but I can think of nothing more insulting. The men I served with were consummate professionals. Yes, they had civilian jobs, but when they put on the uniform, they were soldiers from top to bottom. I didn't have to go overseas, even after 9/11, although there was some confusion about my deployment status. In 2003 my unit was a part of the Iraq invasion, but because I was in Europe competing in the Junior World Championships and my National Guard unit was unclear on how to get me back for deployment, I missed the trip. I didn't even realize it had happened until weeks later. There was some speculation in the media that I had refused to go to war for one reason or another, but nothing could have been further from the truth. If I had been called overseas, I would have done my duty to the best of my ability.

As it was, I was happy to serve as an ambassador for both the U.S. Olympic Committee and the U.S. Army, moving effortlessly between the two, just as WCAP had been designed.

The only time I struggled with the decision was right before the 2000 season. With American companies lining up to piggyback their marketing off the 2002 Olympic Games in Salt Lake City, General Motors put together a promotion to help Winter Olympic athletes. We were all offered the chance to write an essay on why we thought we needed a new vehicle from Chevrolet. I made sure my essay made me sound like a character out of a Steinbeck novel, driving whatever battered car I could keep running, struggling through the tough Colorado and Utah winters. I was also in the National Guard (a point I played up heavily), which meant I had service responsibilities in addition to my bobsled training schedule.

I read and edited and reread the essay many times until I thought it was perfect: inspirational and funny, but also a tearjerker. The effort paid off. Chevrolet marketing executives contacted me and told me I'd won one of the Chevy Tahoes.

It was beautiful—fully loaded with that new-car smell. It was like nothing I'd ever had. I sank into the driver's seat and ran my hands over the wheel. I pushed all the buttons and played with all the knobs. Within a day, I'd touched every inch of it.

Of course, Chevy took pictures and played it up in the media, sending out press releases and making calls. I was

My sister Megan holding me after I broke my femur at 7 months old. I was crazy from the start.

What biography would be complete without a baby picture?

ABOVE: Here I am on the last hill climb of the Bonanza Banzai, an annual Utah bike ride. For the second year in a row, I won. (Of course, the first year I was the only one in my age category.) LEFT: I loved going to Lake Powell. Riding my Jet Ski was by far one of my favorite activities.

ABOVE LEFT: I tried my hand at every sport. Archery was one that didn't stick.

LEFT: While rock climbing with my dad, I learned that there's no easy way to the top.

ABOVE: Here I am representing Park City in the state playoffs as a third baseman.

I spent many summers in beautiful Lake Powell, Utah, by far one of my favorite places on the planet.

It was cool to take your school picture in your Cub Scout uniform.

My dad and I enjoying one of our many camping trips in the beautiful Utah wilderness. We were always on some sort of outdoor adventure.

ABOVE LEFT: My mom and I head up the old Lost Prospector chairlift at Park City Mountain Resort when I am 3 years old.

LEFT: Ski racing was my life.

ABOVE: One of my first ski races. Pretty good angles for a 7-year-old.

ABOVE LEFT: This is what I lived for. Going 140 feet at 75 mph off a jump called Panorama in Crested Butte, Colo.

LEFT: Tristan and me just after carrying the torches at the Snowbird Holiday Torchlight Parade one year.

ABOVE: My mom said I'd be famous someday and wanted to be the first one to have my autograph.

My senior year of football. Little did I know, less than a year later, I'd be representing my country on the World Cup bobsled tour.

Representing my country in a different uniform.

Walking to the start of the World Cup bobsled race in Calgary, Canada, in 1998.

During my first bobsled run, my driver, Travis Bell, did a great job breaking me in.

My teammates and I load into the sled during training at the 2006 Olympic Winter Games.

This shot is taken just seconds after regaining my sight, which changed from 20/1000 to 20/20.

The power of a homemade sign: The very moment that Curve 50-50 was named at the Whistler Sliding Centre in Whistler, Canada.

The Night Train created a sensation when we raced it in Europe. Here we push it in Lake Placid in November 2009 at the Intersport FIBT World Cup four-man bobsled race.

The Night Train in action: me at the helm, Steve Mesler and Justin Olsen in the middle, and Curtis Tomasevicz on the brakes in back, during our final, victorious run at the 2010 Vancouver Olympic Winter Games in the four-man bobsled race.

Winning gold at the 2010 Winter Olympics in Vancouver.

My beautiful niece Annabelle holding my medal the day after I won it.

I was show and tell for my nephew Sten the day after the 2010 Vancouver Closing Ceremony

just thrilled to have a vehicle. Then I got a call from my first sergeant.

"Holcomb, you are a member of the United States Army, and as such you are prohibited from accepting gifts from any person or company that does business with the United States Army," he said.

"I guess General Motors does business with the Army," I said.

"Who do you think makes Humvees, son?"

I didn't answer. But I didn't give the truck back immediately either. I tried to figure out a way to sign the title over to my mom, or somehow transfer the gift so that it wasn't really a gift. But nothing worked. When my first sergeant found out I still had the truck a week later, he called back and let me know in no uncertain terms that I would give that truck back to General Motors immediately or face a court-martial.

Once I heard the words "court martial," "$40,000 ethics violation," and "thirty-year imprisonment," the Tahoe went back and I returned to driving whatever would run.

One of the skeleton athletes, a West Point graduate named Brian Freeman, resigned from WCAP when he didn't make the Olympic team. At the time he was an Army captain with the 412th Civil Affairs Battalion, where he was a better soldier than he was an athlete, and he was a great athlete. Brian received two Army Commendation Medals, two Army Achievement Medals, a National Defense Service Medal, and a Global War on Terrorism Service Medal. He also earned the Combat Action, Air Assault, Parachutist, and Marksmanship Qualification badges and ribbons in Iraq.

Then, on a Saturday afternoon in the village of Karbala, Brian and four other soldiers were ambushed by insurgents dressed as U.S. troops. All five were killed. Captain Brian Freeman was thirty-one years old. He had a wife and two children, ages three and one, when he died.

I think about Brian a lot, his character, commitment, and sense of honor. My every memory is of him helping others, because that was all he ever did. Whether it was walking an inexperienced bobsled driver or skeleton athlete through the nuances of a track or providing encouragement to someone who was struggling, Brian made everyone around him a better athlete and a better person.

Brian Freeman wasn't as well known as Army Ranger and former NFL player Pat Tillman, and his death didn't receive as much attention, but he was every bit a hero and was a world-class athlete. I am proud to have known him and honored to have saluted and called him "Sir."

SIX
Bumps on the Ice

Every life has turning points, moments of decision where the outcome is unknown and the consequences dramatic. Most adults can look back on three or four distinct times when the road of their lives forked and, for good or bad, they had to choose a path. My life is no different. There have been several key decision points when I've made choices that changed my future. Sometimes I have chosen well, and other times I have made terrible mistakes. I hope that my friends and fans can learn from both.

For the 2000–2001 season Brian Shimer picked me as one of the push athletes for his team, which was a great boost (and, in my mind, a great decision). The USA Bobsled Federation and the USOC smiled on Brian. He was the face of the sport in America, and our best hope for a medal in the upcoming 2002 Salt Lake City Olympic Winter Games. But he was also thirty-nine years old, not exactly over the hill in bobsledding, but certainly nearing the twilight of his career. Brian still had the passion and intensity to compete at the highest level, but he understood that Salt Lake would most likely be his final Olympics. He would turn forty that year, the age when reflexes no longer responded as quickly and you had to work out twice as hard just to maintain your level of conditioning. As such, he approached every run with an added degree of urgency.

It was during that time, as I watched Brian become uncharacteristically short-tempered, that I realized every career has an arc, and in order for a team to be successful, each member has to understand where everyone else fits: whose arc is ascending, whose is peaking, and who is on the way down. Sure, everyone wanted to win—it's easy to say that the goal of any team is to become the world champion—but until you understand where everyone is in his career, it's impossible to understand the motivations of all your teammates.

Former Dallas Mavericks shooting guard Jason Terry has spoken about his first trip to the NBA Finals in 2006. It's a great story. The Mavericks got trounced by the Miami Heat in four straight games, losing the last one on their home court. Immediately after the game, Jason was in the locker room with confetti still in his hair from the Heat's celebration. Darrell Armstrong climbed into a hot tub with tears in his eyes. Jason, always the most upbeat guy in the locker room, said, "Don't get down, brother. We'll come back next year."

Armstrong shook his head and said, "It doesn't work like that, Jet. Getting here is hard. You don't just get back like it's nothing. This is no small thing. This is a big thing."

"He was right," Jason said. "For the next four years, I thought about what Darrell said every time we got to the playoffs and fell short."

In 2011, the Mavericks finally won a championship, beating, ironically enough, the Heat in six games. By then Darrell was no longer on the team. In fact, when Dallas captured its first NBA title, Jason and Dirk Nowitzki were the only players left from that original 2005–2006 team. At one point during the final game, when the Mavericks fell behind and it looked like the Heat might force a seventh game, Jason grabbed Dirk by the jersey and said, "Remember '06." They both remembered and came back to win the game, because in 2011 they understood that chances at championships don't come every day.

For Olympic athletes, the Games themselves come once every four years, so lost opportunities carry a tremendous weight. Many things can change in four years. Missing one shot at the Olympic Games can be devastating.

In 2000, I was on the ascending side of my career arc, having been in the sport for only a couple of years. Brian was at his peak. It was now or never for him. So I understood his frustration in the 2000–2001 season when we didn't do as well as we'd hoped.

Throughout the year we experimented with equipment, working closely with Bo-Dyn Bobsleds to tweak designs and setups. Everyone wanted the United States to enter the Olympics with state-of-the-art stuff. Unfortunately, engineering is not a straight-line process. Some changes that would eventually yield positive results created temporary setbacks, as drivers worked with fabricators and engineers to dial in the right combination of speed and control. Those were the kinds of problems we dealt with throughout the fall of 2000 and winter of 2001.

Our finishes were mediocre, and Brian became more agitated with each poor run. Sometimes he would vent at us. Other times he would call the engineers and talk through sled mechanics. The Bo-Dyn upgrades had changed American bobsledding forever, but we weren't operating in a vacuum. German engineers took it personally when we caught up to them, so they doubled their efforts to stay ahead. Losing to better athletes was something the Germans could handle; losing to better engineers was not. Bo-Dyn was in an equipment race with the Germans, and we were on the front lines.

But I couldn't follow the engineering details that closely. I had troubles of my own, something I didn't share with the team or anyone else. My vision was getting blurrier by the week.

—◄○►—

I had worn contacts and glasses for years and thought nothing of it. A lot of my friends and both my parents wore corrective lenses, so it wasn't a big deal, except when bobsledding. On the rides, contacts are a pain—if you've ever seen a can of paint being mixed, that's what it's like being inside a bobsled. You can wear contacts, but it's not ideal given the amount of jostling you endure. But this was about to change during my first year in bobsledding. A local eye surgeon came to the U.S. Olympic Training Center in Lake Placid and offered free Lasik procedures—something that got my attention, since out in the real world, I wouldn't have been able to afford Lasik. After a quick screening it was determined that I would be a great candidate, and so I took advantage of it.

The procedure was a little creepy, but not at all painful. I had to stop wearing contacts for a little over a month prior to the procedure. Then my corneas were mapped out with something called a pachymeter, which is a finely tuned ultrasound machine that measures the thickness and contour of the cornea. Then a topographer created a map of my cornea, including any imperfections like astigmatism. Armed with that topographical map, the surgeon calculated the best ways and places to remove tissue from my cornea.

Lasik is simply reshaping the cornea to eliminate irregularities, and it is done by slicing a flap in the tissue with a laser and folding it over. Once the surgeon had studied the map of my cornea and come up with a plan, I went into a room where I lay back in a glorified dentist's chair. The surgeon gave me a mild sedative, but I remained awake and alert throughout. The creepy part came when they applied something called a "corneal suction ring" around my eye to hold it in place and stop me from blinking. If you ever saw the movie *A Clockwork Orange*, it looks like the torture device used to keep Malcolm McDowell's eyes open. The laser then flashed, creating several bubbles around the cornea to create a flap, just like folding a layer of skin on its side.

Once the incisions were made, the surgeon pulled the flap back. That was a little uncomfortable, but not nearly as painful as breaking an arm or wiping out during a ski run. The anxiety was greater than the pain. Knowing that my eye was being sliced while I was awake and alert messed with my head and heightened every minor pull and tweak that I felt during the procedure.

The second step involved reshaping the cornea by burning off interior tissue with a laser. My vision was blurry during that part, so all I saw was a white light surrounded by orange. The surgeon assured me that this was normal. Once the flap of the cornea was folded over, my vision would be impaired for the rest of the procedure.

After the reshaping of the corneal interior was complete, the surgeon replaced the flap like closing a hinged door. Natural adhesion held the flap in place. That was it. I was given goggles to keep me from rubbing my eyes in my sleep, some antibiotic eye drops, instructions to get plenty of sleep, and some Stevie Wonder–caliber sunglasses to protect my eyes from bright lights.

BUT NOW I SEE

"Healing can take as much as two to six weeks, but you should see progress right away," the doctor told me. "Just keep taking the antibiotics and keep the eyes moistened with drops on a regular basis. Avoid any blows to the head for a while, so no kickboxing." He smiled in a perfunctory way that told me he'd made that same joke so many times even he was sick of it.

"When can I get back to work and see some results?" I asked.

"That's two different questions," he said. "You should be able to get back to work in two to three weeks. It might take a little longer for the incisions to heal. You should see a real difference in about six weeks, no more than eight."

That had been a year ago, and not only was I not seeing better, but my vision kept getting worse. I called the doctor numerous times, and each time I got the same message: keep using eye drops. After a year, I was pouring a bottle of drops a day into my eyes with no improvement.

As we were packing and preparing to head out for the 2000–2001 season—a year that I hoped would be a breakout for our team—the same surgeon who had performed the original Lasik procedure showed up at Lake Placid to give eye tests to all the athletes. I lined up like everyone else to get the eye exam.

When he saw me he said, "Hey, didn't you get a Lasik procedure from me?"

"Yeah," I said, "and I've been calling you ever since because I still can't see. It's been a year and it's never gotten better."

There are some things you never want to hear: your dentist saying, "Oops"; your cardiologist looking at stress test results and saying, "Uh oh"; and your eye surgeon squinting and frowning and saying, "Hmm, that's not right."

We went through the vision test, which I failed. Then he said, "Let's have a look," and he brought the pachymeter back out. The frown intensified as he looked at the images from my eyes. I could tell he was worried, and my heart sank with each passing second. Even though I had known something wasn't right for months, I had always held out hope that a doctor would look at my eyes and say, "Yes, there's a minor problem, but it's no big deal. We'll fix you right up." But the way the surgeon's face darkened, I knew that cheery news was not in my immediate future.

After what seemed like an hour (even though it couldn't possibly have been that long), the doctor came back and said, "I've got some not-so-great news."

My heart leapt, but I tried to remain cool. I still hoped he would say something like, "The Lasik didn't work and we'll have to do it again."

Instead he said, "You have a degenerative eye disease called keratoconus."

"Carrot what?" I said.

He explained that keratoconus was a progressive thinning of the cornea and that the "conus" part of the name referred to the cone shape the cornea would assume as the disease progressed. I also learned that keratoconus was usually manageable through corrective lenses, but that it could cause random eye pain and a loss of depth perception.

"You also might experience moderate to sometimes severe distortion in vision or sensitivity to light," he said.

"How do we fix it?" I asked.

"That's the bad news," the doctor said. "There is no cure. If we manage it properly, we can minimize the disruptions to your quality of life."

He made it sound like managing moderately high blood pressure or diabetes. Then he got to the worst-case scenario.

"If the deterioration accelerates, or we can't manage it through lenses, you might have to have a cornea transplant," he said.

Very few things focus your attention like the word "transplant." I knew about heart and liver transplants, and, of course, stories of kidney transplants—sons giving kidneys to fathers, coaches donating to players, and perfect strangers stepping forward to save a life through donation. They were all touching, but from what I'd seen, the procedures themselves were debilitating. Twenty-year-old heart transplant recipients shuffled around like seventy-year-old men, ashen and drawn. Mickey Mantle had a liver transplant and could barely walk before he died. So when the doctor casually said, "You might have to have a cornea transplant," with all the casual nonchalance of a man going over a grocery list, I got a little freaked out.

He tried to reassure me by telling me this was a worst-case scenario, adding, "We are nowhere close to even considering that as an option now."

What he failed to tell me at the time, and what I wouldn't find out for several years, was that keratoconus should have been discovered in the original Lasik screening. And once it was discovered, the surgery should never have been performed. In hindsight, I believe that only a part of the surgeon's distress came from my condition. A good portion was him wondering how he could have screwed up and sliced into the eyes of a person suffering from a progressive corneal disease.

But given the information I had, I didn't panic. My cornea was thinning, but I should be able to control it with contacts for a couple of decades before having to make any dramatic decisions. By then I would be forty, Brian's age, a time when Olympic athletes retired to other things. It seemed as distant as a tiny star. It annoyed me to know that I would probably wear contacts the rest of my life, but there were worse things that could happen.

Then, as Brian gathered the team together before embarking on the season, I made a decision that would snowball as time went on. I decided not to tell anyone about the diagnosis.

It would be easy to write this off as naïveté. I was twenty and didn't know much about the disease, so keeping the diagnosis to myself helped me to dismiss it as no big deal. Plus, I was in a highly competitive environment where athletes were cut for having toenail problems. I didn't want Brian or anyone else looking at me as the kid with the carrot-sounding eye disease. As long as I could see well enough to do my job, there was no reason for anyone to know that I was anything but normal.

Like most deceptions, this one started innocently enough. I would tell them when the time was right, or maybe I wouldn't. If the doctor was right and we could manage this through contacts for twenty, maybe twenty-five years, there was really no reason to involve anyone else. I was a world-class athlete. I could certainly handle this little challenge on my own.

More pressing to me at the time were injuries that could possibly sideline me for good. I watched another class of rookies go through the same tryouts I had aced, and I watched guys who were superstar football players, sprinters, and triathletes fall out to injury when it came time to push the sled. Hip, foot, and hamstring injuries are the most common in bobsledding. Pushing a sled at a dead sprint on ice for countless reps wears on the lower body. Almost every athlete in the sport experiences some form of lower-body injury during his career.

As we finished the 2001 winter season with a lot of mediocre runs, I felt fortunate to have avoided so much as a single shin splint. But I did have to go back to the eye doctor to get new prescription lenses. I told myself not to worry, although I had to get stronger contacts at a faster rate than I thought I would. As long as I was able to see, I figured I was good to go as far as the Olympics were concerned. Salt Lake would come quickly. Opening ceremonies were February 8, 2002, so when we finished the 2001 World Cup season we had only ten months to get ready for an opportunity that would never come again in our careers: the Olympic Winter Games on American soil.

Throughout the spring, my workouts couldn't have gone better. I continued to train with the team, pushing on the ice as long as we had ice, and on the track once the weather turned too warm. Then the team moved to a special training facility in Atlanta where I lifted weights, sprinted, and pushed.

Then it happened. I was working an "overspeed sprint session," where our coach would use a pulley system to train our bodies to run faster than normal. During one of those sprints, I felt a shock of pain run up the back of my leg. It felt like I had been hit in the hamstring with a cattle prod. Once the initial shock subsided, the burning ache set in. I limped around for a second or two trying to walk it off, but there was no doubt that I had injured one of the largest and most important muscles in our sport. The extent of my hamstring injury wouldn't be known until I saw a trainer and had some tests, but I knew immediately that I was going to be sidelined for several weeks at the worst time imaginable.

I tried to work it out. I did everything in my power to get back into the gym and onto the push track as quickly as possible, but the only way to heal a strained hamstring is to rest it. But with the clock ticking down to the Salt Lake City Games, I didn't have time to rest. Brian needed a full team training every day. The Games wouldn't wait for me to heal, and with this being Brian's last shot, he had no choice.

"Holky, I have to replace you," he said during one of the worst meetings of my life up to that point. Even hearing that I had keratoconus didn't hit me as hard as hearing that my team, the group I had worked and trained and traveled and competed with for more than a year, would go to the Olympics without me. Aggravating the open wound was the fact that these Games were being held in my hometown, a place where I had family, friends, coaches, and former teammates. The sliding track where bobsledding, skeleton, and luge would take place was right next to my high school. Our graduation had been just a few yards from the finish line, a finish line I would now not have a chance to cross during the Olympic Games.

I understood Brian's reasoning, but that didn't stop the hurt. The stabbing pain in my hamstring was nothing compared to the knife-like feeling in my heart.

Then came 9/11, and I wondered if my National Guard unit would be called to war. Like many Americans, I staggered through the days after the horrible events in September, not knowing what to do or say. I watched television and tried to return to as normal a life as possible, knowing that nothing would ever be the same. America was at war, and I was a soldier. If called, I would do my duty. But the wait was maddening.

As days turned to weeks, and weeks to months, with no word from our commanding officer and no Olympic Games to get ready for, I felt the first pangs of something strange and heavy and dark. I could feel myself tumbling. I would sit in the dark or stare at a computer screen as minutes slipped into hours. I didn't want to talk to anyone or see anyone. I didn't want to go outside. It hurt, but not like an injury, more like the ache you get with the flu. I had never felt anything like it before and I didn't know how to respond.

As fall stepped aside to winter, the pain intensified and so did the electricity of the Games. The buzz wasn't confined to Utah. Everybody in the American West stood a little straighter. I had to be a part of it. I just wasn't sure how.

I asked the Salt Lake Organizing Committee if I could be a forerunner, one of the drivers who make four or five runs before each session to make sure the track was ready for competition. They thought it was a great idea, but they had only one concern: "How good are you?"

I had taken my first runs in the driver's seat in March 2000 just for fun. I was a push athlete then, and I knew very well that I wouldn't have enough time to be able to go to the Olympics as a driver, so I stuck with pushing. In the meantime, since I wasn't a big guy and two-man pushing wasn't my style, I figured I would try and get some experience by competing in two-man whenever I had a chance. Pretty much the only time I had a chance was during our national team selection races at the beginning of each season.

At this point, I had actually been driving a bobsled for two years. In the fall of 2000 and 2001, I had competed as a driver, but never finished higher than seventh; not too bad, but not really that good either. It didn't really matter because I was doing it for fun anyway, though it still stings the pride to get beat. I had completed maybe thirty runs in total over the years I'd driven for fun every now and then.

By the time the 2002 Olympic Trials rolled around, I was still ranked seventh in the United States, and just as you would imagine, I finished seventh there too. So when the Salt Lake Organizing Committee asked me how good I was, I didn't really know what to say, although I knew why they were asking. I was good, but ranking seventh was by no means something to be proud of, not to mention the fact that I had only recently made the transition to a full-time driver. Most people knew me as a pusher, so they questioned my ability and commitment as a driver. But they made me a deal: "You can be a forerunner, but you have to have one hundred successful runs without crashing before the Olympics start to prove that you won't be a liability during the competition." The problem was, it was now early January, so I had less than a month to do get it done.

This was a nice way of them trying to keep amateurs with plenty of money and lots of spare time from buying their way into heats and getting themselves (or others) killed. But bobsled tracks aren't like go-kart tracks or even the oval race car tracks. You can't go through three rural counties in America without finding at least one dirt track or go-kart racing center. But there are two sliding tracks in America: the Utah Olympic Park track at Park City and the original American track in Lake Placid. Anyone hoping to become a luge, skeleton, or bobsled driver in the United States has to practice at one of those spots, which eliminates a lot of people from even trying. Also, you can't just show up at a bobsled track and buy time. You have to have some background and knowledge of the sport or you'll be politely shown the door. The fact that I lived in Park City and knew most of the track workers proved to be a significant advantage, one that had nothing to do with skill or desire. I just happened to live in the right place—nothing more.

Of course, growing up in Park City and knowing everybody at the track didn't make me a good driver. If I'd been awful, it would have shown up quickly and I would have been out of the sport. But after hundreds of runs as a pusher, I felt like I had a sense for what it took to guide a sled down the track. Once I jumped into the front of my own sled, I realized that I was like the guy who thought he could fly a jet because he'd ridden in the jump seat a couple of hundred times. There was a lot more to it than met the eye.

Grabbing the D-rings for the first run on my hundred-run quest was like gripping my future. It felt firm and deep and purposeful. Then, in less than a second, I had to maneuver the sled into position to enter the first turn and all those self-congratulatory, metaphoric thoughts flew behind me like loose ice. The only conscious thought I had for the next minute was: One hundred runs without crashing? Holy smokes, what have I done?

The second trip was a little less terrifying than the first, and the third even less than that. By the fourth or fifth run I began to focus less on reacting once I had the sled out of position and more on getting into the right position from the start. The tendency early was to overdrive. Gravity has hardwired our brains to two-dimensional thinking when it comes to navigation. Even though highway turns are slightly banked, it's never more than a degree or two. So if you take your car into a 180-degree turn at seventy miles an hour, you're going to have to rotate the wheel hard to keep from running off the road. But bobsled tracks are fully banked, so when you hit that same kind of turn, you do so 90 degrees up an embankment. If you turn too much from that position, you slide the sled down the track too far and you lose time and control.

I also had to learn not to overcorrect. If I did get the nose of the sled pointed down the track, the tendency was to pull on the opposite ring to straighten out. But sliding on ice isn't like driving on asphalt. Overcorrecting a turn could result in hitting a wall or bottoming out, neither of which is good for your time or the sled.

The other problem I had was finding people to push. Because I was on a mission to complete my hundred practice runs in thirty days in order to be eligible to be a forerunner for the Olympics, I needed somebody to ride in the back for balance and weight. My passengers didn't have to be athletes. I didn't want a race-timed start. I just wanted to get going with someone behind me to create the sensation I would experience in a competitive run. So I recruited everybody I could find— my dad, track workers, friends. I would approach anybody and say, "Hey, you want a ride?" Very few people turned me down, although a few were apprehensive when they learned that I was a relatively inexperienced driver. Still, I averaged more than three runs a day, which doesn't sound like a lot, but given the wear and tear on your body and the number of g's you pull in each turn, it was an exhausting period.

Undeterred, I finished my hundred practice runs in record time, getting faster and more confident with each trip. But that made the Salt Lake Games even tougher. I was there. I was working. I was making runs on the track . . . but I was not a competitor.

The opening ceremony was the worst. Seeing my friends, my teammates, and the people I had known and whose world I had been a part of for years walking in with their cameras to the cheers of the home crowd was like a dog whistle to the dark demon that was taking root in my soul. When the demon took over, I could barely lift my head. It felt as though a weight had been placed on my shoulders and chest. Even breathing was tough, and every movement hurt. Lifting my cheeks in a forced smile felt like bench-pressing two hundred pounds, and I would do whatever I could to avoid having to talk.

When I wasn't forerunning for the bobsled events, I watched bits and pieces of the Games. These were my dear friends, and it would have been rude and selfish of me not to throw all of my support behind them. My ex-girlfriend Tristan Gale—that dear childhood friend and the person I had dragged with me to push tryouts in the first place—competed in the inaugural women's skeleton competition. With her hair dyed red, white, and blue, Tristan appeared to be having a great time, even though her runs occurred while it was snowing. At five feet two inches and 108 pounds, she thought she needed a clean track to compete. The snow would slow her down more than others, or so she thought. Tristan also wasn't expected to do well because she had never medaled before in any World Cup event. Just getting to the medal podium would have been an incredible achievement.

When she crossed the finish line of her second run and saw that she had won the gold medal, she high-fived every fan lining the bottom of the track. Then she stood on the medal podium in a spot where we had thrown snowballs at each other as adolescents and put her hand on her heart as "The Star-Spangled Banner" rang out over the cloudy sky. I shared her tears of joy that afternoon. It was the one time during the Games that my demon took a break and allowed me to feel truly happy for a friend.

Then my team with Brian Shimer won the bronze medal in the bobsled competition, while the other U.S. driver, Todd Hays, the man I had pushed for in my second year in the sport, won silver. It was the first time Americans had won Olympic medals in bobsledding in forty-six years, and we had two teams on the podiums.

As happy as I was for both Todd and Brian, I couldn't shake the darkness. Four years was an eternity in my mind. I was twenty-one years old. Four years before I had been in high school. Where I would be four years hence was something I couldn't imagine.

As tough as it was to watch my team on the medal stand without me, that was the moment when I knew that I could never experience these feelings again. To know that I was going to the Olympics, I had to control my own destiny. I couldn't have someone cut me from the team again. I had to be the person who made those decisions.

I was a driver. And that was where I had to stay.

SEVEN

Grasping the D-Rings

Bobsledding isn't like football. An offensive tackle can't suddenly decide to play quarterback, no matter how long he's been in the league. Linebackers don't show up at summer camp and say, "Hey, I think I'll move to wide receiver this year," and the center can't announce that he's moving to tailback. In most sports, the position you learned, developed, and perfected is where you remain. There are a few exceptions, however. In basketball, a good point guard can transition to shooting guard, and a big forward can move to center. Pittsburgh Steelers wide receiver and Super Bowl MVP Hines Ward played quarterback at Georgia before moving to wideout in the pros, and a fair number of NASCAR crew chiefs are former midlevel drivers. But third-year Major League Baseball first basemen don't suddenly move to pitcher, and veteran goalkeepers don't wake up one morning and announce their intention to start playing wing.

That is where our sport is vastly different. Because almost nobody in America grows up on a bobsled track, all our athletes enter as pushers. From there you gain experience and either stick with pushing or you become a driver. Todd Hays and Brian Shimer both followed this path. They answered the open tryout calls like everybody else, went through the workouts, and made their respective teams as push athletes. According to Brian, "They sent me a plane ticket to Lake Placid and the promise that I could travel, train, and possibly make an Olympic team. I had no idea what I was getting into."

Like a lot of the athletes the federation recruited in 1985, Brian had never seen a bobsled race in person when he first tried out for the sport. But it didn't take long for Brian (like me) to fall in love. And, like me, he realized a couple of years into his career that if he wanted to remain a bobsledder, he needed to place his destiny and success in his own hands. He needed to move from pusher to pilot. He needed to hold the D-rings.

For those unfamiliar with bobsledding terms, the D-rings are the steering rings that allow the bobsled to change direction. The rings are connected to a rope that is attached to the steering mechanism (all sled designers have their own proprietary design for the steering), which is attached to the front axle, and when the driver pulls the left or right ring, the sled moves to the left or right accordingly. It is primarily the combination of the push-off, the design of the sled, the weight of the team, and the driver's abilities that affect the outcome of a race. The only acceleration comes from the four athletes pushing at the start and gravity pulling the sled down the hill. The driver controls where the sled is on the ice so it's hitting the perfect line on the track. Unlike a driver of a car, one thing the bobsled driver doesn't do is stop the vehicle. The person in the back of the sled is also called the brakeman, because he pulls the brake when the race is over (and only then; the brake is not used at all during the run).

—◅○▻—

After being cut from Brian's team, I found myself at a crossroads. At twenty-two years old, I had already traveled the world competing in an electrifying sport. I was also a service member with the Utah Army National Guard. I hadn't been sidelined because I wasn't good enough; I'd been replaced because of injury, a familiar story to athletes from every sport. There would have been no shame in calling it a career, getting a job, and moving on with my life.

But I was not getting worse as an athlete; if anything, I was just coming into my own physically. I had matured as a person and as an athlete, and my sense of what was and was not a good bobsled run had been heightened by training. My mind worked in hundredths-of-a-second increments now. I was the guy who should be breaking the new kids in, not the one sitting on the sideline. Most twenty-two-year-olds are just beginning their professional lives. Some are getting their first jobs. Plus, I had always aspired to be an Olympic athlete. It was what I had gone to school to train for and what I had always seen myself being. Bobsledding was the vehicle to realize those dreams. Walking away seemed unfathomable.

At that point in my life, self-reflection was not in my nature. I was always looking ahead and thinking about the process of achieving my goals: the next run, the next race, the next day of training. But the injury and forced exile from my hometown Games forced me to take stock of where I was and where I was going.

Plus, I think the months and years immediately following 9/11 changed the way everyone thought about their lives and careers. We were all jolted out of a self-centered complacency and illusion of security on 9/11. Like everyone else, I woke up to the realization that life was not a linear equation. All the "if/then" propositions I had come to accept as gospel pre-9/11—if you dedicate yourself fully to a goal, then you will achieve it; if you seize opportunities and work tirelessly, then you will succeed—became curved and inert in the aftermath. The course of any interesting life is always filled with twists and turns and outlying data points that average into the arc of our external existence. Very seldom do you know when you are making a decision that will have a lasting and monumental impact on everything else that follows.

I knew I had much more to give and so much more to achieve in bobsledding and found the thought of never competing again and never quenching my thirst to be an Olympian incredibly unnerving. There was no time to waste. No man was promised tomorrow. I also had this eyesight thing that might someday force me into retirement (although thoughts about my keratoconus remained vague and fleeting at that point, like plans for retirement or nursing care once I became aged and infirmed). Since I already had more than a hundred runs as a driver, some in practice and others as a forerunner for the 2002 Olympic Games, I announced that I would henceforth be a bobsled driver.

The only problem with that sort of announcement is that nobody cared. ESPN didn't cover my proclamation. There was no press conference, no formal ceremony, and no federation representative putting his arm around me and saying, "Steven's our guy." I've gotten more response to tweets stating my intention to go to Starbucks than I got when I declared my conversion from push athlete to driver. When I told the coaches, their reaction was blasé. The only real change was that I was no longer included in pusher meetings and was added to the roster for driver meetings. For all practical purposes, my big announcement was a party for one.

If I wanted to drive, I needed to prove that I could get the job done. But in bobsledding, nobody is lining up to give you equipment or an opportunity to race just because you ask. The USA Bobsled and Skeleton Federation dictates who gets the Bo-Dyn sleds, and at the time of my announcement there were some accomplished, veteran drivers waiting in line for those. Officials weren't going to hand over a prized commodity like a Bo-Dyn sled, now the crown jewels of our sport, to a rookie driver. I was on my own.

By borrowing some money from my father and the owners of a local ski shop, Cole Sport—the same folks who gave me the luge action figure as a gift when I was a kid—I was able to go in 50/50 on a two-man sled with a fellow named Mike Kohn, another pusher who had decided to become a driver. And then, once again, fate, providence, or divine intervention played a significant role in my success. Had the Olympics not been in my hometown in 2002, and had I not been so driven to be a part of those Games that I worked to become a forerunner, exactly no one would have noticed my ability to pilot a sled down a track. Even though the forerunner's job is to test the suitability of the track before competition, a lot of people saw me drive during the Games. Also, as expected, after the 2002 Games, Brian Shimer retired from driving and moved into coaching. Todd Hays, the silver medalist from the Salt Lake Olympics, stayed put as the driver of USA-1 sled, but USA-2 was open for a new driver, which was Joe McDonald, the driver of USA-3. If my calculations were correct, I figured Todd would probably retire after 2006, when he would be thirty-seven years old. That would shuffle the deck once more, leaving USA-1 open for the person who stepped forward now and proved himself. I had every intention of being that guy.

To do that, I had to learn to do something I hated—play politics. Like every team environment, whether it's the local Little League, a major college football program, or a U.S.

Olympic team, once you reach a certain level, everyone is skilled. The differences in ability are razor-thin. So who gets a shot and who doesn't often hinges on who can play the political game correctly. Certainly, it's not difficult to find the star running back on a football team. But when it comes to who makes the punt team, the kid whose dad made a substantial donation to the athletic department has a leg up.

Bobsledding is no different. The guys who play the game, who maneuver through the unseen minefields surrounding the various federations and committees, get more of a look than the guys who aren't as politically savvy. And, as is the case in any sport, egos play a role. Stroke the right person at the right time and your life is a lot easier. But say the wrong thing—even something innocuous like telling a joke someone finds off-putting, or failing to respond with the proper enthusiasm to someone's idea—can put you on the bad side of a decision maker and make your life uncomfortable at best, miserable at worst.

Unfortunately, politics has never been one of my strong suits. I have always been straightforward with everybody and more or less oblivious to nonverbal political cues. I steered clear of controversy and tried to avoid all the inevitable internecine wars that break out in any organization. Most of the time that attitude worked in my favor, but there were times that it left me alone on an island, especially when I returned to the sport as a driver.

Fortunately, both Brian and Todd vouched for me as a committed team player. Their blessings gave me a foot in the door. After that, it was up to me.

I did well in the early competitive heats, never getting to the medal stand but never embarrassing myself either. I learned with each run not just what it took to be a good driver but what it meant to be the leader of a team, the person responsible for the outcome. The push athletes get the sled off to a winning start, but it is the driver who has to finish. It is the driver who takes the buzzer-beating last shot every time, who drives the team down the field for the winning score, who hits the game winner in the ninth, or who takes the anchor leg of every relay. Equipment and conditions play a role, but I understood that the quality of my team's performance rested with me. As pressure packed as that realization was, I was ready for the challenge.

The dark spells that had befallen me after I failed to make the 2002 U.S. Olympic Team slipped into hiding as I worked my way back onto the ice. I found that focus and purpose kept the demon at bay. But as my disposition brightened, the rest of the world continued to grow increasingly dark—my eyesight was getting worse by the month.

The process was gradual—blurry words on a page a mere month after getting a new prescription, or finding that I couldn't follow sports on television because my eyes couldn't pick up the ball—but my vision was definitely and steadily declining. My descent into blindness was not so dramatic that I thought about it every day. Like anyone with worsening sight, I went to the optometrist on a regular basis and got stronger contacts. It was more of an annoyance than something I feared. I didn't think about the keratoconus on a daily or even weekly basis. It was vague and distant, like the ghost of a ship on a foggy sea, out there somewhere but not close enough to be real. Or so I thought.

The one conscious concession I made to politics was not telling anyone I had keratoconus. Since it wouldn't affect my performance, why admit to any weaknesses? If I had acid reflux or irritable bowel syndrome, I wouldn't have shared that news either, because it had no bearing on my ability to drive a bobsled. And even among your own teammates, friends, and fellow Americans, you never want to telegraph your vulnerabilities. To say, "Oh, by the way, I have a degenerative eye disease that is slowly robbing my vision. Not to worry, though, it won't be a problem for many years," would have been like announcing that I had leprosy.

I had just gotten back into the sport as a driver. The last thing I wanted to do was send signals that I was damaged goods. Some people wouldn't understand and others would blow it out of proportion. I was sure that if I told anyone, the rumor mill would churn it up until word spread that I would be blind by the end of the week.

My sight wasn't that bad, I reasoned. I would keep the keratoconus to myself and simply get stronger contacts as I needed them. I would tell everybody about the disease in fifteen or twenty years when I finally retired and it didn't matter anymore. But until that time, I wanted the world to believe I was invincible.

EIGHT
Fine Lines

I faked the swagger in the beginning. At the top level of
any sport, you have to project a certain air—the confidence of a champion. But when you're the newly
minted leader of a team, sometimes you have to pull that aura
out of your backside. Weakness on the World Cup circuit is
like blood in a shark tank. If my opponents (and a lot of my
fellow Americans) had sensed that I was unsure of my new
role as a driver, or that I lacked the confidence to compete on
the big stage, I would have been eaten alive.

Throughout the 2002–2003 season, I "juked the jive"
as the snowboarders say. I was fortunate enough to win the

America's Cup Circuit in Park City, Lake Placid, and Calgary, which gave me a berth to replace Joe McDonald in USA-2 on the World Cup circuit. At my first World Cup race in St. Moritz (followed by events in Germany and Italy), I became a master faker, an inexperienced newcomer who learned to act like I'd been at this for years. The longer I assumed the false persona of a confident driver and team leader, the more confident I became in both my driving and leadership. It was as though I became the character I had created or the character became me. Somehow the two of us dissolved into one.

The on-the-job training that came with a full World Cup schedule didn't hurt. Each competitive run improved my confidence as well as my speeds. At first I didn't know what I didn't know—things like how the sled should feel as I set up for a turn, or what a controlled transition from one turn to the next looked like. I didn't realize how much I fishtailed through my early runs until our coaches played them back for me on tape. Improvement requires taking an unflinching look at your mistakes and talking through what is needed to correct them. I did that every day of the 2003 season and even into 2004.

I also became more comfortable in my new role as the up-and-coming driver for Team USA. The hierarchy of bobsledding demanded that I set the tone for my team. Every unit responds to the attitudes and actions of its leader. If the head guy shows a lackadaisical work ethic, the men in his charge will eventually slack off. If the leader shows a lack of respect for equipment or presents himself in an unprofessional manner, the rest of the men on his team will be equally un-kempt. But if the leader shows he cares about all things big and small, and if he sets the example through his work and dedication, demanding the same from his teammates is easy.

As I've gotten older, the fundamentals of leadership have become second nature to me. It is much easier now to set the example, communicate the standards, and demand ex-cellence from those around me. But at age twenty-three, twenty-four, and even twenty-five, that wasn't always the case. I thought I could compartmentalize, separating my on-track time from every other minute of my life.

I realized that wasn't the case during one of my early trips to Germany. After one of the practice runs, all the sliding ath-letes hit the town and enjoyed a little Bavarian hospitality, which included more than a few local beverages. Most guys in their early twenties don't have to worry about enjoying them-selves in the pubs every now and then, as it's considered a part of the maturation process—but as an athlete and leader of a team, I had to be held to a different standard, one I didn't understand and resented.

The next morning I felt like I'd been dragged down the autobahn for a few miles. "You okay?" my brakeman asked.

I'm not sure what I mumbled, but it was something like, "I'll be fine," which couldn't have been further from the truth. That day went about as well as you'd expect. Our runs hovered between lackluster and amateurish. I drove like a grandfather.

Later, I could sense the disappointment in my team and my coaches. There were hushed murmurs behind my back and a general sense of malaise from everyone. I didn't think much about it at the time because I was nursing a wicked hangover, but later, as I reflected on that time, I realized that I could not bifurcate myself into Steven Holcomb, Bobsled Driver and Steven Holcomb, Twenty-Four-Year-Old Looking to Party. My every action set a tone.

I didn't stop drinking after that (maybe I should have), but I did moderate my behavior around my coaches and teammates. We still went out to dinner and recreated together, but I was much more cognizant of my role. Just as I had seen officers in my Army National Guard unit maintain a professional distance from the enlisted men, I began to pull back a little, trying less to be one of the guys and more the leader of our small group.

It was tough. More than once I had to go one-on-one with one of my guys—correcting my pushers and making sure that they understood what we were doing and why we were there—which was difficult for me at first. Most of the pushers were either college athletes or military guys—men my age or older with social experiences I'd never had—so asserting myself as a respected leader required some maneuvering. Thankfully, I had some very professional and motivated teammates who didn't need a lot of cajoling from me. More often than not I would encourage and make constructive suggestions, but there were a small number of times when I had to tell someone that he needed to get his act together.

As 2003 raced into 2004, the year of the Summer Olympics in Athens, Greece, we showed steady improvement in each race with plenty of top ten finishes but no surprise wins. Because Todd Hays was still driving USA-1 and doing quite well, we had the luxury of being on the track but out of the limelight.

The same was true of 2005. By then I was twenty-five years old: prime time for an Olympic athlete. It was time to take the next step.

-◄o►-

I play golf (although not very well) and I love it. Like downhill skiing, there is a solitude and vulnerability on the golf course that you don't find in other sports. When you're skiing, it's just you and the mountain. You are totally exposed with no teammates to fall back on, and no excuses for how you perform. And no matter how good you are, or how fast you made it down on your last run, you can always improve. Things could be going along perfectly and in an instant you catch an edge or get out of position and down you go. Golf has the same qualities, although without the danger. When it's your shot, you can't hide. No matter how well you play, you know that you could play better. Of course, you could also play much worse. And even if you're having the best round of your life, one lapse in concentration, one lazy swing or bone-headed decision, and your score can skyrocket.

As I've gotten into golf, I've also noticed that there are a lot of extremely good players who have never been shown on Sunday telecasts and who most people couldn't pick out of a lineup. When I'm on the driving range at an event, I watch good amateurs and tour players, and it's difficult to tell them apart. Many amateurs have what seem to be flawless swings. The ball explodes off their clubs, flying long and high and straight, and I say to myself, "Wow, this guy is incredible. Why have I never heard of him?" Then I realize that I am a casual observer, and as such I can't see the chasm between a good amateur and a major champion. On the driving range, the margin appears so small, but in reality, the difference between a good amateur and the best pro is larger than the gulf between a hacker like me and a good amateur. I'm simply not immersed enough in golf to spot the subtle nuances that differentiate an average pro from a world-class champion.

The same is true in bobsledding. Most people can watch a race and see no difference between the team that finishes first and the team that finishes twenty-first. Both appear to push well and the sleds don't bang the walls or crash. What the viewer can't see are the minute differences: the cleanliness of the start or the lines the driver puts the sled on to maximize speed and create a slingshot effect as the sled glides through the apex of a turn. Nor can anyone see the focus of each man on each team during a run.

I didn't appreciate how deep and dark the rabbit hole of focus is at the top level of sports until I was in the driver's seat. At the top level of any profession, the difference between first and tenth is minuscule. By 2005 I had experience, but everybody on the track was experienced. I had speed and strength, but no more or less than the other drivers. I had good equipment, but the gap in quality on that front had narrowed to almost nothing. What I didn't have, and what I had to have to up my game to the next level, was the focus of a champion, the intense mental toughness that made Michael Jordan and Tiger Woods unstoppable in their prime.

In three years of driving, I made steady progress, but I never medaled. Our team wasn't making terrible mistakes, but USA-2 simply wasn't as sharp or as fast, and I wasn't as focused and mentally tough as some others on the ice. It's the equivalent of a golfer being content to make pars while the winners make birdies and eagles. Pars aren't bad, and you can make a good living playing even-par golf, but it isn't good enough to win. Our runs were solid, but they weren't great.

I knew I had to make myself better, but it was becoming increasingly difficult to focus on bobsledding when I couldn't focus on the world around me.

It wasn't unusual for someone with glasses or contacts to need a new prescription every year or even once every six months. The eyes weaken and a slight adjustment has to be made. But I was finding that my sight was getting noticeably worse by the month. Whenever I was home, I would research and contact ophthalmologists in the hopes that someone somewhere could arrest the rapid degeneration. No longer was I thinking in terms of having to make a decision about my eyesight in a couple of decades, after I retired. At the current rate, I would have to do something in just a few years, if not sooner.

It was during that time prior to the 2006 season—a year when I was scheduled to compete in my first Olympic

Games in Torino, Italy—that I first thought, *Oh my God, I could go blind.*

I considered telling my coaches and teammates at that point, but as I pondered that option, it dawned on me how awkward it would be to confess my disease now. I'd been diagnosed with keratoconus years before. I had known about the condition and where it was leading when I'd made the decision to become a driver. To come forward now and say, "Oh, by the way, guys, I have this degenerative eye disease that is robbing my vision at an alarming rate, but I've known about it for years," would have been a slap in the face to everyone.

Plus, I was on the cusp of finally realizing the dream I'd had since I was old enough to answer the question "What do you want to do when you grow up?" I'd always wanted to be in the Olympics, to walk into a stadium filled with cheering spectators behind the American flag, and to represent my country in a sport that I loved. Now, with that dream only a few months away from becoming a reality, I could not fathom telling the world (and my fellow competitors) that I was going blind.

It was selfish. I should have told someone. If I'd confessed earlier and explained why I hadn't said something sooner—*"I didn't tell you because I was told that it was a manageable condition that wouldn't affect me for another twenty years"*—then I might not have struggled later on. But like anyone with a secret, once I kept it for a year, it became easier to keep it for two years, and then three. Only when my eyesight deteriorated to a point where I could no longer function normally did I realize what a box I'd put myself in. And because the only lengthy conversations I'd had about my disease had been with myself, I always came up with the most horrific scenarios for what would happen if I confessed now. My demon told me that I would be tossed from the Olympic team if I said anything. I would be ostracized and shunned for having kept vital health information from my coaches and teammates. Certainly, I would be taken out of the sled immediately.

Those thoughts were crazy, but at the time, the burden of my disease and the weight of keeping it a secret skewed my perception. I was so fearful of losing the Olympics—the one thing I had worked for my whole life—it was easy to convince myself that I needed to lie to everyone.

Besides, the one spot where I felt most at home, where I could maintain some semblance of control, was the sliding track. I loved the ice and being surrounded by its whiteness, a blinding chasm completely absent of color. And the sled had become a part of me, like an elongated second skin. When everything else in my world was slipping away, the sense of oneness I felt with the sled never faltered. It was my instrument, and I played it with all of my remaining senses.

Bobsledding with limited vision wasn't that tough because you don't see much anyway. You are surrounded by white ice on three sides. Going eighty miles an hour, the only thing you see is the occasional fan or flag or patch of blue sky zipping by overhead. All drivers are sight-impaired on the track, even if their vision is 20/20.

It was off the track that my problems were more noticeable. Because I wore contacts most of the time, people didn't realize how bad things were getting. But on the few occasions when I had to put on glasses, it was impossible to hide. Bullet-proof glass wasn't as thick as the lenses in my eyewear. When someone would occasionally walk in on me after I had taken my contacts out, I could sense their shock. I would always yank the glasses off my face, quickly but not in a way that revealed my eagerness to hide them. Then I would look at the blurry figure and carry on a conversation as if I were seeing his every expression.

I'm sure my sense of hearing improved naturally as my sight grew worse, but I also worked at it. Bluffing required me to concentrate on every sound. Who was standing across the room? What was happening on the television in the corner of the restaurant? I knew the answers, not because I could see but because I became hypervigilant in listening.

The biggest con I pulled came right before leaving for Torino. All athletes had to take a sight and hearing test to be cleared for international competition. Thankfully, this wasn't like a drug test. Everyone had to read from an eye chart without glasses, but we all lined up together in a very informal and loosely controlled setting. So prior to the test, I walked up to the chart and covered the biggest letters with my hands.

"What's it say now?" I joked with the others in line, a moment of levity, or so it seemed. I was actually memorizing the chart. When my time came, I covered one eye and then the other and read away, getting as deep as anyone before misfiring. But I couldn't see a single letter. My recitation came from memory.

That bluff bothered me, but not enough to come clean. It wasn't cheating the way taking performance-enhancing drugs was cheating, or so I told myself. The eye test was a joke—one of those things a bureaucrat in a cubicle had come up with to keep us busy—and every athlete treated it as such. Of course, the others who didn't take it seriously had no trouble passing it. I was the only one who had to cheat to keep my darkening world a secret.

—◦—

The USOC gave me two tickets to Torino, so I took my parents (who still didn't know about my condition). Mom and Dad had seen how missing the Salt Lake City Games affected me, and they had been my biggest advocates as I transitioned from pusher to driver. Mom had done her best to lift me out of despair as the Games ripped through our hometown, and she had cheered my every finish—even the bad ones—as I learned to drive. Dad had put his life in my hands, climbing into the sled behind me as I was getting in my initial runs. He had believed in me enough to help fund my first sled and never stopped encouraging me.

Seeing their faces when I told them that they had tickets to the two-man and four-man events in Italy was worth a million white lies and fudged vision tests. My biggest fans would see me compete in the Olympic Games, even if I couldn't see them.

The problem was logistics. Beyond the two family tickets, we were on our own. Any other family member or friend who wanted to make the trip would have to find their own credentials, and everyone, including our parents, had to make their own travel and accommodation arrangements. Since the Olympic team isn't announced until a week or so before the Games begin, a lot of the travel stuff is guesswork. If your parents book a flight and a room and you don't make the team—tough. If you make the team and they haven't booked, they're scrambling to find accommodations.

Mom was surprised that the committee wanted to brief her before we left. I'd been given brochures that explained the drill to family and friends, but the spiel was a little harsher when delivered in person. Your child is not going to Italy to entertain you. He is going to compete in the biggest event of his life, so leave him alone and let him focus on his job, or some variation of that message. Mom was upset that she might not see me at all, even though interrupting me in Torino was the last thing on her mind. She had lived the Olympic dream just as much as I had, maybe more. My parents had sacrificed mightily to send me to The Winter Sports School. Dad had built the furniture for the school for free in exchange for my tuition, and Mom gave up weekends and vacations and any modest luxury so that I could go to ski races. It was my parents who had instilled in me the message, reinforced through love, that I was destined to be an Olympian. Seeing me fulfill that dream filled my parents with indescribable joy.

I had no idea what to feel. The hubbub of getting to Torino, checking into the Olympic Village, and going through orientation kept me too busy to feel much of anything other than sensory overload. There were logistical instructions— this is how you will get to your venue, this is when you will depart, these are the credentials you must keep with you at all times—and instructions for when and where to eat, sleep, and walk. We were given a list of rules for the Athletes Village, including who could come and go. I thought I'd seen airtight security on some of the Army bases where my Guard unit drilled, but those were public parks compared to the guarded compound that was the Athletes Village. Nothing moved in or out without going past layers of large men with big guns.

My first sense that this was finally and really happening came the night of February 10, 2006, as the entire U.S. delegation prepared to ride into Stadio Olimpico di Torino for the opening ceremonies. Dressed in matching uniforms, we gathered outside the main stadium gate as 35,000 people cheered for the most elaborate show I'd ever seen. Skaters and aerial acrobats put on a breathtaking display. Up close their costumes reminded me of the Power Rangers, but the choreography of their performance was spectacular.

When our time came, and the words "United States" were announced, I knew what Brian Shimer had been talking about when he said he'd gotten "hooked" at the opening ceremonies of the Calgary Games. The roar was deafening and what looked like a million flashes went off as people throughout the stadium snapped photos. Like everyone, I waved and smiled and tried to drink in every second of the experience. I didn't see all the people in the stadium as well as others, and my view of the fireworks might have been a little blurry, but at that moment I couldn't imagine how anything could top this.

I had to wait eight days from the opening ceremonies until the bobsled competition, but the time flew by. In addition to practice, I watched as many events as I could. But my mind was never far from the Cesana Pariol track, a 1,435-meter serpentine labyrinth with nineteen turns and three hundred feet of elevation change. Top speeds were a shade over eighty miles an hour.

The two-man races came first. My pusher, Bill Schuffenhauer, and I got behind right out of the gate. Our first run was 56.15 seconds, nine-tenths of a second behind the Germans, which might as well have been an hour. Making up three- or four-tenths in the remaining three runs was a tall mountain: coming back from almost a full second down was akin to scaling Mount Everest in a Speedo.

We never improved our position after the first run and finished the two-man race fourteenth, exactly the middle of the pack. Andre Lange and the Germans won gold, with Canada and Switzerland taking silver and bronze. Todd and his pusher, Pavle Jovanovic, finished seventh; respectable, but not what Todd had hoped for in what everyone expected to be his final Olympics.

Four days later, things were much different. The four-man race was always the event where I felt we had the best shot. That prediction turned out to be correct. With my mom among the throng of fans cheering from the grandstands, our four-man team prepared for our first run with every intention of ending up on the medal stand.

Bill Schuffenhauer, my two-man teammate, stood beside me along with Lorenzo Smith and Curt Tomasevicz. Curt had been a football player at Nebraska, while Lorenzo was a West Point grad and Army air defense artillery officer in the World Class Athlete Program. Bill was the most experienced guy on the squad, having been on Todd's silver medal team in Salt Lake City.

Track conditions were perfect. We had a solid first run until my right side push bar didn't come in fast enough and we hit the wall, slowing us down and causing us to skid. The push bar didn't retract all the way either—the kind of frustrating mechanical problem that can cost you a chance at a medal—but we were still in good shape. Our time of 55.46 was two-tenths behind the Germans, who led after the first heat. I still believe that without the mechanical failure we could have been in the top three.

Todd and his USA-1 team also had a good showing, nipping us by three-hundredths of a second.

The lineup for the second heat was based on how you finished the first. Since we were in sixth place, we went out sixth from last, right behind Italy-1 and Germany-2, which meant we were playing to a full house of rowdy fans. The Italians came out with gusto in support of their athletes. Going out so closely behind the home team and the Germans (whose second team was always expected to beat us) electrified the environment even more than normal. I felt chills, and not because of the cold. This was what the Olympic experience was all about.

Our second run was 55.50, good enough to keep us in sixth place but still a couple of tenths slower than the Germans. Four-tenths was too much to overcome, but we still had a chance to climb into medal contention. Unfortunately, everybody stepped it up in the third heat. Even though we logged our best time, 55.14, we dropped to seventh place, right behind Todd and USA-1.

But that worked to our advantage when it came to the final heat. Once again the starting order was based on position, so we went out right behind Russia, but immediately ahead of Todd and his team. We would set the American time to beat.

My pre-heat pep talk was fairly subdued. I told our guys to look around and drink in everything they saw. This was going to be our last run of these Olympic Games. "Let's go out with all we've got," I said.

Our start was great, one of our best, and I felt certain that we'd hit the first time mark in a good position. The track was a little slower for the final heat (just like in skiing, fresh snow will impact times). I still felt as though we were keeping pace. When we crossed the finish line, I saw that I was right. Our final run was 55.35 for a total of 3:41.36.

After the final team crossed the finish line, we were still sixth, not a medal, but a huge accomplishment for our team and a great step for me in my first Olympics.

The USA Bobsled and Skeleton Federation and USOC took notice, especially since Todd announced his much-anticipated retirement between the first and second days of the Olympic four-man race. That left the driver's seat for USA-1 open. Officials from the federation called a meeting with me. "You've never won, but you're it," they said. "You're the new face of American bobsledding. Time to step up your game."

Indeed it was. Unfortunately, my secret weighed heavier by the minute. How could I be the face of American bobsledding when I was going blind?

NINE
Bright Lights, Dark Corners

The psychological term is "cognitive dissonance," a fancy, clinical phrase for the strain caused by holding two conflicting ideas in your mind at the same time. It's possible for a person to believe that two or more mutually uninhabitable events can live side by side—I don't believe in God, but I'm going to Heaven; I know she's cheating on me, but we're going to live happily ever after; I'm going to lose weight and eat this pizza—but the emotional toll eventually overloads the psyche. Your brain can referee this sort of thing for only so long.

My cognitive dissonance couldn't have been clearer. I had to prove myself worthy of being the leader of USA-1, the face of American bobsledding, while harboring a secret that couldn't be hidden forever and a condition that was only getting worse.

Even without the keratoconus, no one was sure how I would respond to the pressure of being the go-to guy for U.S. bobsledding, especially the officials at the USOC who controlled the purse strings. The bureaucrats in charge of our Olympic teams weren't interested in spending a fortune to fly and house and feed and equip a team that had never medaled in a single World Cup race, especially with the Beijing Summer Games coming up in eighteen months. All the focus was on China, and rightfully so. Guys like Michael Phelps were expected to make history. To get any attention at all, I had to prove myself quickly. Competing in the 2006–2007 World Cup season was not a given. Funds were tight.

While I was focusing on upping my game in the sled, I also had to deal with my worsening eyesight and the fact that I still hadn't told anyone that I was almost certainly going blind. I met one ophthalmologist after another, and the message was always the same: "No, there's really no cure, but you are a perfect candidate for a cornea transplant."

The word "transplant" became a knife, shredding all hope with cruel and precise efficiency. According to experts, the transplants would need to be done one eye at a time with a recovery period of between eighteen and twenty-four months for each procedure. Four years of surgeries and rehab, followed by

BUT NOW I SEE

continued maintenance: eye drops and checkups and a lifetime of anti-rejection medication. Even if the transplants promised to make me as good as new, I would be out for at least one Olympic cycle and a minimum of four World Cup seasons, which might as well be forever. Had I healed up perfectly and been able to come back, my spot would have been taken by the next up-and-comer in the sport. I would be a has-been just when I'd gotten started.

But transplant surgery carried another gut-wrenching complication. My eyes could not be jostled or banged around, no blows to the head or other excessive trauma, all the things that were commonplace in a bobsled run. I didn't get beaten like a fighter, but we all got rattled around like ice cubes in a tumbler. That sort of thing could cause newly implanted corneas to detach, leaving me irrevocably blind. A transplant might seem like a perfectly reasonable option to all the doctors who described it—"Really, it's much more common than you think. We have a very high success rate"—but it meant that I was out of the sport, and, as a result, out of a reason to get up in the morning. Out of a sport where there was instinctual order and where I knew how to anticipate and react to the slightest shifts—a place where I was the nucleus of the team, the race, and the future. The only place I understood completely and where I knew that I belonged.

A lot of people would view this as an easy call. "Sure, okay, you can't drive a bobsled anymore, but at least you wouldn't be blind!" And in the broadest sense, they would be right. Piloting a sled down a track is, in the grand scheme of things, not all that important, especially in the context of revolution and up-heaval and all the uncertainty in every aspect of life today. But none of us live in the grand scheme of world history. Each life has its own precious assets, built through toil and time. And when those assets are stolen, it can shatter that life and leave the empty sense that every hour has been a waste. That is especially true in sports, which has a special appeal to the better nature of man, sort of like life in fast-forward with the volume on high. Sports encapsulate everything: dreams, desires, talent, sweat, grit, agony, and thrill. Sports also exaggerate the vagaries of life: a gust of wind slowing a skier a fraction of a second, or a tiny fleck of debris catching an edge and shattering a dream. Fate, luck, chance, and destiny all factor into life, just as they play a role in sports. So while it might be easy for an outsider to say, "What a no-brainer! Have the surgery and regain your sight," that person cannot possibly understand what it's like to be so singularly focused on a goal, so consumed by the dreams you've had since childhood and the countless hours you have devoted to reaching a certain point that you can't imagine existing any other way. What would I do if I had to walk away from my dreams? Who would I be? Olympic athlete was not what I did; it was who I was and all I had ever thought about being. The idea of having that snatched away from me at the moment I was reaching the pinnacle of my sport was something I could not accept but could not ignore either.

Some diseases can be hidden and, if you work at it, forgotten. Keratoconus is not one of those. I was about to reveal my secret for the first time.

The first person I told was my mother, not in some cathartic moment of confession but in response to some shocking news of her own.

We were all at home for a family dinner. My sisters, both married by then, had come to Mom's with their husbands. It was a lovely evening filled with light conversation. Then, with dessert on the horizon and the pops and hisses of percolating coffee drifting in from the kitchen, my sister Stephanie casually asked, "Mom, how are your eyes?"

Mom waved a dismissive hand and gave a half-smile, a gesture meant to indicate that everything was fine—nothing to worry about and silly to even bring it up. But I knew this to be her way of deflecting. Whenever she had a problem, something personal and deeply uncomfortable, she always offered the same "oh, gosh, gee-whiz, it's nothing" smile and easy flick of the hand, as if shooing away an annoying insect.

"Oh, it's fine," she said, reinforcing her gestures and confirming to me that something must be terribly wrong.

"What's wrong with your eyes, Mom?" I asked.

"Oh, I have this thing where the corneas are thinning," she said. "It's not that big a deal. I just have to keep up with it."

She must have seen me turn white, because her next words were, "Steven, are you okay?"

A shock ran through my body and my legs began to tremble. I stood and said, "Mom, can I speak to you for a minute?"

The rest of the family shared puzzled glances as Mom and I strode to the kitchen. Once out of earshot, I said, "What do you have, Mom?"

"Oh, it's nothing to worry about," she said. "I've had something called keratoconus for about five years. It's a degenerative . . ."

"I know what it is, Mom. I have it too."

Her face fell, her eyes pained by instant recognition. She had kept her condition from me because she didn't want me to worry. Little did she know that I was going through the same thing, keeping my condition a secret for more complicated reasons.

"How long do you think you have?" I asked.

"How long?"

"Before you have to have a transplant," I said.

"I don't know," she said. "Hopefully, never, but if I do it will be a long time. I'm managing it pretty well."

Then her face changed. I could see the horror as it dawned on her why I'd asked. "Oh, Steven," she said. "I'm so sorry. I didn't know."

I looked away and batted back tears. "Neither did I, Mom," I managed to say.

—◦—

My first race driving USA-1 was at the Olympic track in Calgary, competing for the World Cup. While a trip to the beautiful plains of Alberta was technically a trip abroad, it was hard to tell the difference between Calgary and Omaha, Nebraska. When you are on the road, focusing on sports, one city tends to look like the next. But it didn't matter where we were: without a decent finish, my first outing would likely have been my last, at least during this 2006–2007 season. It was then that I realized what eighteenth-century English poet Samuel Johnson meant when he said, "Nothing focuses the mind like a hanging." I had to run well or this would be it.

Johnson also said, "What we hope ever to do with ease, we must learn first to do with diligence." Those words could not have rung truer. I had been diligent and determined in my efforts to become the best driver possible, spending every waking hour and much of my dream-filled sleep shaving fractions off my times. Now I had to turn all those hours of toil into victories and bring a different mind-set to the track, a quiet cockiness and complete immersion in each run, where every nerve and synapse fired for a singular objective.

The Canada Olympic Park houses one of the most famous sliding tracks in the world, not because of the Olympics or any World Cup event that has been held there but because it's the track that was used by the Jamaican bobsled team, as portrayed in the movie *Cool Runnings*. At 1,474 meters long, with fourteen turns and four hundred feet of vertical drop from start to finish, the track is tough but fair. With a good start and a clean run through the Omega Combination (turns six, seven, and eight, which formed the shape of the Greek letter omega), I felt like we had a chance to do great things.

I had never been so quiet and calm before a race. The ice was the one place where I could put everything else in a corner—the disease, the distractions, the future—and for a couple of minutes embrace the world I knew best, a place where my immediate future was still in my control.

The runs in Calgary went better than a lot of people expected, but I felt like they were on par with where we were as a team. Each start was a nanosecond faster than its predecessor, and every turn felt cleaner and more precise than the one before. More than anything our confidence had manifested into a quiet calm, each member of the team finding his personal zone where the runs came to him. I had become so comfortable at the starting line, the slick sweat on my skin wicking through the fabric of my race suit, the crisp air finding the inevitable gaps in coverage. Every second on the track felt exactly as it should.

When the final heat concluded, the board showed USA-1 in second place.

We had won the silver medal in the first race of the year. No one other than the men on our team thought it was possible, but we all believed it was the first of many. Our second-place finish turned out to be a feat that sent a powerful shock wave through the bobsledding community because it didn't look like a fluke. Every run was solid and we carried ourselves like a team that could contend every time we hit the track.

I had never felt more comfortable in my life. Every ounce of focus, every nerve in my body, and every synapse in my brain had responded with a singularity of purpose, an almost artistic effortlessness that I knew existed but had never experienced for myself. The mystics (and snowboarders) called it Zen. For me it was the Art of the Ice, the moment when my driving was no longer driving but finding our center in a run, like a sculptor who no longer thinks about his hammer and instead pulls the image (and his soul) out of the stone.

The stillness that comes with being completely absorbed in a task, even at eighty miles an hour, can only be found through relentless repetition and an impassioned quest to find perfection. During our runs in Calgary, nothing else mattered. I wouldn't have been able to tell you my sisters' names before the start.

Bolstered by our good showing in Canada, we moved on to Park City, where we finished second again. Then in Lake Placid we kept the streak going with yet another second. That was when we realized, "Holy smokes, we're in the running for a World Cup title," which had never been won by an American two-man team. We immediately applied for emergency funding from the USOC so we could afford to get through the next few races, even though there was no guarantee that we could compete all the way through the winter.

As impressed as the bobsled federation guys were by our showing, the USOC still had a Summer Olympic Games to fund, so we got just enough to send the team to Europe without any coaches. Thankfully, one of our coaches lived in Switzerland and was able to take the train to Cortina, Italy, to meet us for the next race of the season.

On a shoestring and adrenaline, we arrived at the Eugenio Monti track, one of the oldest sliding tracks in the world (and the one that James Bond skied down in *For Your Eyes Only*), ready to continue our streak. The track meanders through a pine forest with twelve of the sixteen turns named after villages in the area. It's quiet and quaint, not exactly the spot for a breakout, but that is exactly what we gave the Italians. By the time the weekend came to a close, my two-man and four-man teams both won gold.

Two races and two wins—a clean sweep.

I felt exhilarated like never before, but it wasn't as though I had reached my goals and could relax. The winner's circle felt like home. This was where I belonged. I wanted more, and I wanted it quickly.

The next race was in Germany, where we finished second. Then it was off to Torino, where the Olympics had been held only a few months earlier. The place looked a lot different without the thousands of fans and the electricity of an Olympic Games. A fair number of fans showed up for the event, but nothing like what we'd experienced a few months prior. The outcome felt much better, though. Instead of finishing sixth as we'd done in the Olympics, we swept, winning both the two-man and four-man competitions. Six stops and twelve races into the season, we had three silver medals and five golds.

Our roll continued. We were on the medal stand in almost every event. Far from being "under the radar" anymore, we became the team to beat. And our expectations grew with our performances. We expected to medal and win more than we lost. Once you break through and taste victory, you will do whatever it takes to stay on top. When the last event closed in the spring of 2007, we walked away having done what no one thought possible: a U.S. bobsledding team was the overall champion. We had won the World Cup.

I should have been on top of the world, and when I was at the track that's exactly where I was. I felt like Superman during and immediately after the races. Each win brought on a high unlike anything I'd ever experienced. The only rush that came close was when we blew stuff up during Army National Guard drills. But even that didn't compare to seeing a "1" by our names after a race.

Unfortunately, the vast majority of life took place away from the track. That was where I struggled.

I've heard a lot of athletes talk about the difficulties they have coping with the banalities of everyday life, especially after the bright lights go out and the rush of victory fades. Not only are athletes physically exhausted after their seasons, but many struggle with feelings of depression that range from mild (overeating and parking in front of the television during the off-season) to manic (wrestling alligators and riding bucking bulls to try to recapture the thrill, as Chad Ochocinco did when NFL contract negotiations broke down). Adrenaline and endorphins have been wildly intoxicating for millennia. Roman emperors used to ride through the gates of the city to cheers and chants after battle, but they kept a slave by their side to say, "Remember, you are just a man."

Fame has always been a fickle mistress. But my affair with the demon was darker still, because each victory served as a reminder that I was a fraud, a liar by omission. I knew that I was driving on borrowed time, but I wanted to forget or ignore that fact. Unfortunately, by the time the season ended, I couldn't see the cheering fans. My trips to the ophthalmologist had increased to once a quarter, and every three or four months my sight deteriorated to the point where I needed new lenses. I knew the end was near, and yet I continued to do whatever it took to keep my secret, even though doing so made me feel empty. My window was closing quickly, and my mind could no longer process the cognitive dissonance of my dual life. On the track, I was invincible. Off it, I was a broken man falling ever further into the depths of despair.

—◁o▷—

Twelve specialists told me the same thing. After a while it felt like a recording: "You're out of options. It's time to put you on the transplant list." Some couched it in broader medical terms, while others tried to soft sell it by saying things like, "Your current lenses might last longer," and "There is no uniform time frame for sight loss," but they all ended up in the same place: I needed a transplant. Everyone swore that keratoconus was not genetic. The fact that my mother and I both had it was, according to all the doctors, a great cosmic accident. Her disease had nothing to do with mine. No matter. I was legally blind. How I got here was irrelevant.

I had also stopped going out with friends and teammates because of the awkward moments. Someone would speak to another person across the room and I would be lost, not knowing if that person was waving at me or speaking to me or even looking at me—his face was a blur; or a game would be on the television in the corner and I couldn't watch. The prospect of questions like, "Hey, Steven, you want to throw darts?" or "You want to play Madden?" petrified me, so I did everything I could to avoid them. I lived like the boy in the bubble, only my bubble was sight. Arm's length was about as far my field of vision got, and even then the fingertips were blurry. Beyond that, the world was like a murky swimming pool, a collage of dark shapes moving in and out of a tiny sphere of blurry light and color.

Imagine going out with friends and not being able to read a menu or the sign on the bathroom door; imagine not being able to flag down a server or see the bartender. After a while you stay away. I used the ubiquitous white earbuds of an iPod as my nonverbal stop sign, walling myself off from human contact even in a crowded room. I also immersed myself in whatever I could place right in front of my face, usually a laptop that I propped on my chest. It blocked anyone from seeing my expression and sent an unmistakable message: leave Holcomb alone.

I tried to pretend that this was the new me: the quiet assassin, the badass Terminator who stays quiet until called upon to wipe out the competition. But soon the personality I pretended to have became the personality I had. My actions became habits and the habits became who I was. Somewhere deep inside, I knew the person who blew off his teammates wasn't me, but I also knew that I had become very good at keeping others out of my shrinking world.

The demon of despair (and more) came heavy and often in those days, and I would greet him with the silent resignation of an exhausted and abused lover. It is hard to explain to someone who has never suffered through bouts of serious depression how bad it feels and how much you welcome the hurt. There was a comfort in the pain, a familiarity in the weight it carried. The ache in the muscles, the throbbing in the deepest recesses of my brain, the taxing effort it took to get out of bed or even to raise my head, and the never-ending sense of panic, like an army of invisible assailants beating me with a million ball-peen hammers: I wanted and needed it all to stop, but when it came, in a perverse way, I welcomed it. The demon's logic always seemed flawless—*You're going to have to walk away from the sport, Holcomb. Retire just as you hit your peak. Surgery is your only option.* Those thoughts made me swirl deeper into the darkness, because that reality was too much to bear.

My disconnect with others grew worse over time, and my circle of friends dwindled. I sensed that my teammates thought I was an egomaniacal ass. In reality, I was crying silently for help every day.

The need for athletes (especially men) to be tough made it very hard for me to keep friends during that time. My best friend was a woman named Katie Uhlaender, a skeleton racer whose career mirrored my own. Katie was a track athlete who got into skeleton in 2003. At the Torino Olympics Games she finished sixth, just like me. Then, also just like me, she came out in the 2007 season and surprised everyone by winning the World Cup.

Part of our friendship stemmed from the mirror-image success we had in our respective sports, but also I found her to be someone I could talk to easily. Having grown up as the only boy in a house full of sisters, I found Katie to be like a member of my family. Her dad, Ted Uhlaender, and I hit it off great. He was a former Major League Baseball outfielder and coach with the Cincinnati Reds and Cleveland Indians, so we never lacked for things to talk about, even though I never did a lot of talking. Even with Ted I was guarded, still hiding my deep, dark secret.

Katie was the only friend I felt comfortable opening up to. When I reached my breaking point, I confided in her about my disease, although I didn't come totally clean. I didn't tell her how quickly I was losing my sight or how far my life was spinning out of control.

"I'm really down," I said. "I don't know what to do."

"You've got to suck it up," she said. "You gut it out and do what you have to do."

She meant no harm. Most people have little understanding of eye disease and even less about depression. I found that anytime I mentioned my eyesight to someone, he or she always tried to one-up me: "Oh, you think you have bad eyes, I can barely see the road at night," or "Your eyesight can't be worse than mine. My vision is 20/60." At 20/200 you're legally blind. By the time I confided in Katie, my eyesight was 20/500 and getting worse.

The other thing I've found is that when you're experiencing depression, people tend to tell you to cheer up, or buck up, or

man up—some form of euphemistic pep talk. It is wonderful
that these people take the time to help out a friend, especially
one who is having a bad day, but for the seriously depressed
person, the "suck it up" bromide is like trying to fix the *Titanic*
with a caulking gun. Katie had tried to cheer up a friend, to
build me up and tell me that everything was going to be okay,
but I was far beyond that.

I forced a smile and told her "thanks," but the demon's
hold was too strong. There was only one way to get rid of him.
There was only one way out.

—◅○▻—

It happened in a hotel room during an event I was attending
in Colorado Springs. I had spent the evening socializing with
sponsors and supporters, fans who wanted to talk about the
sport and how great it was to have me in it. I'd smiled and
laughed and lied with effortless abandon, leading them on
and letting them believe that the money they were investing,
and the time and effort they were putting into me, was well
worth it. Each falsehood flowed easier from my lips, but like
water dripping in a bucket, the weight continued to build.
People were putting their hard-earned money and their faith
in me. My teammates were entrusting their lives to me, and
I was foolishly keeping a dangerous and devastating secret.
One slip, one wrong move, one crash, and I would be responsible for possibly injuring an athlete who had no clue about
the conditions under which he was competing. I had wrapped

my entire existence up in the quest to be an Olympic champion, and now, with that opportunity right in front of me, I realized I couldn't reach it because of a crippling, damning disease.

The bottle of choice was Jack Daniel's—a big one, just under a liter. I loved the taste, rough and sturdy, like an unpolished block of wood. One glass over ice begged another and then a third. By the fourth, the ice had melted and the demon had drifted into the distance like a dull echo. It was now or never.

The plastic bottle with its child-proof white top seemed far too small to hold seventy-three pills, but that was the number. I poured the small, blue pills into my palm, cupping my hand to keep them from falling. One or two on the floor wouldn't make a difference, but I felt the need to be tidy about it. I didn't stare long, didn't ponder. There had been enough of that, enough agonizing, enough sleepless nights. The demon's logic prevailed. All the paths of my future led where I could not go, did not want to go. Only one path remained open. In one quick motion, I threw the pills in my mouth. By now, with the ice a faint memory on my numbing lips, the glass seemed superfluous as well. So I grabbed the bottle of Jack Daniel's and tipped it back, pulling a long swig of it to wash the little helpers down. I was intoxicated and my body was tingling. I had taken all seventy-three sleeping pills and thought I would sleep forever.

I half lay and half sat on the bed, sipping from the bottle as I slipped away. I have no idea how long I remained upright.

The lights were out. I would be found the next morning, both bottles nearby. No note. None needed. It was better that way.

There will always be legions who say, "I could never imagine suicide. How could you do that?" For most of my life I was one of those who thought, *No way, not me. Things could never be that bad.* That is an easy argument to make from the comfort and safety of a normal emotional existence. Certainly, I felt that way for many of the years that I struggled with keratoconus. But the strains of a dual life, and the agony of your dreams becoming out of reach, chip away at you like a hatchet on a giant tree, bit by bit until even the sturdiest base begins to teeter. It doesn't happen overnight. Depression isn't something you catch in the wind one day and get sick the next. It is a gradual, degenerative process, much like my keratoconus. And just like my blindness, I chose to battle the demon on my own, without telling anyone or seeking help from others. I failed. By the time I threw those pills into my mouth and finished off the liter of Jack Daniel's, suicide tasted like candy, a treat that would once and for all end the suffering that had become such an integral part of my existence.

No way was I supposed to wake up.

The next day, I opened my eyes and found a blanket wrapped around me and a pillow over my head, dust mites dancing on the beams of a bright midmorning sun through a nearby window. I lay still for several minutes and thought about what had happened. Half the dose I had swallowed should have killed me, even if I'd washed it down with water. The fact that I'd taken seventy-three pills and downed them

152

with a bottle of Tennessee whiskey should have been overkill. Instead, I was very much alive and invigorated, having had my best sleep in years. There were no signs of sickness, no vomit or bile on the bed or the floor. I wasn't even hungover. I felt great.

I had never given much thought to miracles prior to that morning. Like a lot of cynics, I'd thought that those who looked for miracles or "God's will" in everything were inherently weak people searching for either an excuse for their own failures or a cosmic rationale for the good things that happened to them. You made your own miracles through focus and work, or so I'd always believed. Besides, if God bestowed miracles on the world, why did He choose so poorly? Weren't there starving kids in some African hellhole who needed His attention a lot more than the middle-class white people who always claimed to have been blessed by this or that miracle? And what had happened to all those Old Testament "miracles" where God destroyed cities or sent plagues of frogs or made rivers divide in half? Even a little water to wine or leprosy healing would have been more miracle-like than some of the stuff I'd heard people chalking up to the Almighty.

But if waking up that morning was not a miracle, what was it? How could I explain what I'd done and what I felt now? The more I pondered the matter in the cool, still silence of the day, the more I realized that miracles are not seismic events. Smiting Gomorrah isn't the only miracle evident and available to us. There are wonders and mysteries in everyday life that we simply accept without calling them miracles, when, in fact, that is exactly what they are. The earth hanging in the only orbit around the sun possible for water, oxygen, ozone, and carbon to thrive and meld and interact so that life in all its many forms can flourish is an unfathomable miracle. Yet mankind has taken the existence of the planet and the stars for granted since we crawled from the caves. Snowfall on the mountains insulating hundreds of thousands of species underneath, and all the interaction between those species, surviving, feeding, protecting, reproducing—violently, instinctively, wonderfully—these were overwhelming feats, things that, no matter how they developed and evolved, could only be described as miracles.

Was a young man with a natural predilection to sliding sports growing up in Park City within sight of the only American bobsled track west of Lake Placid any less of a miracle? Or how about that same young man coming of age at the dawn of American dominance in bobsled design? Was that anything short of miraculous?

I had been told often that I was "destined" for greatness. Growing up as an athlete you hear that a lot, so much in fact that most athletes never take the time to let the words sink in. What is destiny? And assuming that I was destined for greatness, destined by whom or what, or for what purpose? For the first time in my life I really took the time to think about how often I'd heard the word "destined" applied to me, and I thought about the earnestness each person had shown in telling me about my destiny. But if it were true, if I was, in fact, destined for things larger than myself, the question was, "What now?"

I didn't have the answer. I was still blind, wearing the strongest contact lenses made, and they were not strong enough. But I was alive, sitting up, breathing the crisp Western air, clear headed and alert when I should have been dead. There was only one word for that: miracle.

—<o>—

In the Ice House in Calgary, the hardest words I ever uttered were when I told Brian Shimer, "I'm blind." Verbalizing it to a coach—someone who had been in the sport for a quarter century and who knew the impact of what I was saying—made it real. It also allowed me to finally break character in front of him. When the "Terminator" façade fell, it crumbled in a wave of emotions. Before, I had used the character as both a mask and a shield, a way of intimidating my competitors and hiding my human frailty. Once I let someone in, I felt completely exposed.

The demon had grown smaller, but I still had to battle him. In the time between the night of pills and whiskey and the day when I finally told Brian about my disease, there were moments when the darkness crept in and I was tempted to welcome the hurt once more. I fought the good fight during those times and brushed back a repeat of my worst days.

What I didn't realize until the moment I spoke to Brian was how great the weight of my secret had been. Like the

Chinese proverb of the man whose children add a stone to his bag each day until one day the man falls over dead, never realizing that he bore the added burden of the stones, I did not appreciate the cumulative effects of my secret. When I finally shed that baggage, I felt like I had thrown a marble yoke from my shoulders.

Shimer stood motionless, stunned when I laid it all out for him. After a few minutes he nodded slowly. It came together for him. My retreat into isolation, my preoccupation with Internet research, the lack of interest in watching anything—it all made sense now. We talked. I told him about the specialists I'd seen, the uniform prognosis I'd been given, and how a transplant and retirement were my only options. I told him that I hadn't said anything before because the speed of the deterioration had surprised me. "It wasn't supposed to happen for years, maybe decades, if ever," I said. It was a rationale for keeping such important information a secret, and not a very good one.

I didn't tell him about the pills. That would stay with me.

Finally, Brian said, "We're going to fix this."

I smiled. "Did you hear the part where I said I'd seen a dozen specialists?"

"Yeah, but there's got to be something out there," he said.

No one could fault Brian's optimism. Even through the sport's bleakest years, he had been the most upbeat guy in the world. I didn't have the heart to tell him that this was one time when positive thinking wasn't enough.

"Look, I don't know if it'll do any good, but I'm going to

call Scott Stoll," he said. "He's always on the cutting edge of medicine. If there's something out there, Scott can find it."

Scott was a medical doctor in Pennsylvania who had been on the 1994 Olympic bobsled team in Lillehammer, Norway, with Brian. I'd met him a couple of times. He seemed like a good man, but he was also a back and neck specialist, not exactly what I needed. Still, I didn't want to dampen Brian's enthusiasm.

"Yeah, see what he says," I responded.

Then I told the team about my condition. All the fears I had harbored about how they would react turned out to be unfounded. No one shunned me. No one leapt at the chance to replace me. In fact, it was exactly the opposite. I was embraced. My teammates and coaches and friends rallied to my side and promised to do everything in their power to help me. Even the USA Bobsled and Skeleton Federation got involved, putting the word out that one of our own needed help. It wasn't long before Brian called.

"I spoke with Scott Stoll, and he's going to call you," he said.

Not long after that Scott called. It was clear that he didn't understand the advanced nature of my keratoconus. Once I explained to him where I was, he said, "Oh . . . well . . . let me see what I can find."

Weeks turned into months, and summer slipped into fall. I was, for all practical purposes, retired, even though there had been no formal announcement to that effect. Then I got the call. Scott had found someone, a doctor in Beverly Hills who was experimenting with an "off-label" procedure to strengthen the cornea with intense infusions of vitamins, specifically riboflavin, combined with ultraviolet light.

"What's off-label?" I asked.

"It means that it's not FDA-approved."

"Like cannabis or those herbal cancer treatments you get in Peru?"

"No," Scott said, "like aspirin."

"Aspirin?"

"Yeah, aspirin isn't FDA-approved for heart attacks, but everybody knows it helps, right? Take an eighty-milligram aspirin a day if you have a heart condition."

"Right."

"Well, that's an off-label use. Aspirin is a pain medication. The heart benefit is secondary."

"So this vitamin treatment is like aspirin for my eyes?" I asked with more than a little skepticism in my voice. We both knew I needed more than a couple of aspirin.

"It's worth seeing him," Scott said.

He had a point. A dozen specialists had given me no sense of hope. Seeing one more doctor couldn't hurt, and it might help. I wanted to be open and easy to work with, especially since Scott had gone to so much trouble. Plus, it was an excuse to go to Beverly Hills. I assumed that I would get the same answers I had everywhere else and that I would say, when it was all over, "I told you so."

TEN Holcomb C3-R

On December 21, 2007, I walked into the office of Dr. Brian Boxer Wachler with no expectations. Rejection numbs the senses, and I had very few feelings left to hurt. Once you've hit rock bottom, you have no further to fall. Nothing can shatter your outlook or attitude. Dr. Boxer Wachler wouldn't be the first to tell me that I was going blind; he wouldn't be the first to say, "You're a great candidate for a transplant," or "There's nothing we can do"; and he wouldn't be the first person who didn't understand the turmoil I'd been through. But at least I got a short vacation to sunny California out of the deal.

Dr. Boxer Wachler looked exactly like what you'd expect from a Beverly Hills ophthalmologist: single-digit body fat, perfect tan, a haircut that cost more than an iPhone, and teeth so white they needed a warning label. He also looked like an athlete. After a few minutes of small talk, I found out that he had rowed crew at UCLA and then at the University of Edinburgh in Scotland. He also rowed on the Scottish national championship team in the Henley Royal Regatta and still competed in amateur races around the country. I asked if he had ever tried to make the Olympic team. "I wasn't quite that good," he said. "Not like you."

We talked a little longer, not about my eyes but about racing and our shared experiences. It was a refreshing change. Every doctor I had seen prior to this trip talked almost exclusively about my disease. In Dr. Boxer Wachler, I found someone who was interested in what I did and what I thought. We were both big believers in visualization—running a race over and over again in your mind, experiencing every second in intimate detail: the wind and the crowd, the heavy breathing, the tension in your muscles, and the thrill of crossing the finish line—long before getting to the starting line. He said, "I really believe that the more detailed and focused you can be in your visualization, the more likely you are to realize those experiences."

I agreed. When we won our first race I wasn't surprised, because I had already seen myself finishing first hundreds of times in my mind. But visualization had a downside, one I didn't share with the good doctor. For years I had perfected

the art of envisioning myself on the Olympic podium re-
ceiving the gold medal. But in the next minute, I saw myself
completely blind, unable to walk without assistance, inca-
pable of ever watching a movie, seeing a football game, or
staring at a beautiful woman again. Both those futures had
filled my mind until they could no longer coexist. That was
when I hit my breaking point.

After a few more minutes of chitchat, our conversation
drifted into choppier waters. I told Dr. Boxer Wachler about
half of my dreams: the half where I was Olympic champion.
I told him how much I had sacrificed to reach that goal.
Then I told him about the failed Lasik surgery, how my keratoconus had been missed, and how I had been diagnosed late
and how quickly my eyes had deteriorated. I told him how
much I had struggled, and how I could no longer jeopardize
the safety of the men in the sled with me. I explained the
trauma that occurred during every bobsled run, saying, "It's
like shaking a bag of peanuts, only we're the peanuts."

He nodded and asked some pointed and probing questions. I got the sense that he empathized with what I was experiencing, and that he understood how devastating it had
been for me to walk away from everything I'd spent my life
building. The caution light flashed bright when we ventured
into things like how I felt when I realized that I might never
race again, and what prompted me to ostensibly retire. I didn't
tell him everything, but I shared enough for him to connect
with my pain.

Then he said something that caught me off guard. "I have

worked for years to help patients just like you," he said. "The good news is you don't have to have a cornea transplant."

"Wait, what?" I said, not believing what I'd heard.

He shook his head and said, "I wouldn't recommend an invasive procedure, especially given what you do."

I'd conditioned myself to believe that a transplant was my only option. To have someone tell me otherwise, in such a matter-of-fact fashion, sent shock waves through my body.

"But I've had a dozen doctors tell me a transplant was my only option," I said.

He smiled. "You see that diploma on the wall?"

"No," I said. "I can barely see the wall."

That earned a much-needed laugh. Recounting all the bad news and what it had done to my life had also called up some of the dark sensations of the past. Any time I spent too much time talking or thinking about the subject, it felt like my soul was in free fall inside my body. Just hearing Dr. Boxer Wachler chuckle helped pull me back.

"Well, I graduated from Dartmouth medical school," he said. "So the MD by my name is the same as those other guys who told you they wanted to cut your eyes."

"Yes, but there were a dozen of them and only one of you," I said.

He smiled. "Isn't that why you're here?"

Good point. I'd come to Beverly Hills chasing a miracle, my second one in a year. But unlike others who came miracle-hunting in California—wannabe starlets who ended up waiting tables at the Olive Garden, or worse, shooting seamy digitals in Encino—I was prepared for rejection. My guard remained high, even after Dr. Boxer Wachler told me that there was, indeed, a different and better way to restore my sight.

"You are a perfect candidate for C3-R," he said.

I told him I thought C3-R was the robot from *Star Wars*, another less-than-hysterical joke, but one that kept the mood light enough that I didn't become an emotional basket case.

"C3-R is 'cornea, collagen, and cross-linking'—that's the three C's—and the R stands for riboflavin. It's kind of an acronym that I wrote out on a United Airlines cocktail napkin on a trip with my wife," he said. "Basically, it's a noninvasive procedure I developed where I apply a concentrated dose of riboflavin into your corneas, and then hit your eyes with ultraviolet light to activate the vitamin. It won't reverse the deterioration you've suffered so far, but it will arrest any future problems. In other words, it won't make you better, but you won't get any worse."

"That's it?" I asked. I only knew of riboflavin because of the few times I'd eaten salty convenience store chips and figured they were so bad for me that I should read the nutritional label. No matter how much saturated fat, cholesterol, sodium, sugar, and carbohydrates junk food has, you can bet it contains at least two percent of the recommended daily allowance of riboflavin.

"I'm not sure how much the other doctors explained to you about keratoconus," he said. "The cornea is like the curved windshield of a race car or a speedboat, only this windshield is made out of collagen. The collagen fibers are bowed like an arch, which gives the cornea its structure. Thickness and shape are critical because the cornea refracts light and accounts for about two-thirds of your total optical power."

I knew most of this, but found it soothing to hear Dr. Boxer Wachler going through it in such simplistic detail. So many of the doctors I'd met spoke in prefabricated sound bites, like they were giving speeches they had memorized in their first years of residency. Once the monologue was over, they said, "Do you have any questions? Good." And they were gone. At least Dr. Boxer Wachler and I were having a conversation. He was taking the time to walk me through my disease, a tutorial I hoped would end with an explanation of how riboflavin would cure what every other MD had said was incurable.

"Sometimes, the collagen fibers become weakened because there aren't enough antioxidant enzymes in the cornea," he continued. "Free radicals are being created by cells, which is normal, except in the weakened cornea there aren't enough enzymes there to absorb them, so they start breaking down the collagen. The collagen fibers become weak, just like some chemicals might weaken the structural integrity of a windshield and it will warp, or lose its shape. When the collagen fibers that make up the cornea get weak, the cornea bulges."

That was a perfect encapsulation of keratoconus, although I'd never heard it described exactly that way. The disease was, for lack of a better term, a hernia of the eye. But unlike other hernias, there was no way to repair a cornea, which, as Dr. Boxer Wachler pointed out, was just a series of perfectly formed collagen fibers.

I think he could see that he had my full attention, but he also sensed that this was trodden soil for me. He quickly pivoted from the freshman biology lesson to a personal story. "My goal throughout my career has been to find new, noninvasive ways of helping patients," he said. "The human body has a fantastic capacity to heal and there are so many nonintrusive ways to strengthen and encourage the body's own resources. Since I became a doctor, I've been striving to find those ways."

His genuineness struck me hard. Just as I had spent my life in quest of a medal, Dr. Boxer Wachler had spent his career in search of new ways to save the eyesight of those who were speeding toward blindness.

"I was reading a study in a medical journal about some intriguing results from experiments where collagen fibers were treated with riboflavin," he said. "The studies indicated that the fibers were strengthened significantly when infused with a concentrated mix of what most people commonly call vitamin B2."

He paused and leaned forward, smiling as if he were about to deliver a punch line to a joke. "The most intriguing aspect of the study," he said, "was what happened when the treated fibers were exposed to extended ultraviolet light. A thirty-minute dose of light on top of the riboflavin turned weakened collagen fibers into almost super fibers. They became better than they were in their original form, almost like something out of a comic book."

My mind was racing, imagining characters like Spider-Man or the Incredible Hulk, once ordinary people, zapped with some strange radiation to create super powers beyond their wildest dreams.

"The more I read about this collagen treatment, the more I thought, wow, maybe this would work for a cornea," he said. "So I began experimenting in the lab along with several experts until we came up with the right mixture of the riboflavin and ultraviolet light. That was back in 2003.

"I performed my first procedure in 2004. I can't tell you who it was because he's a famous movie producer, but the results were beyond my expectations. We were able to arrest the keratoconus immediately."

Four years he'd been doing this! How many doctors had I seen in four years who had told me there was no hope? How much agony had I gone through? And how many others had lost their sight or undergone painful transplants?

My interest turned suddenly to anger. "Why haven't I heard of this until now?" I asked, barely able to contain the quiver in my voice.

"I've been trying," he said. "I made my first peer presentation in 2004. When I showed the results to other professionals, I thought everybody would be thrilled. This really was a breakthrough. But the reaction I got was exactly the opposite. I was like the bad guy in the Western movie who walks into the saloon and everything stops. Doctors came up to me afterward and said, 'There's no way that works.' Even though they had my results in front of them, they wouldn't believe it.

"I realized later that they didn't want to believe it. Transplants are big business. They're very profitable. A lot of doctors saw me as somebody upsetting the apple cart. So instead of getting the word out, I spent a couple of years fending off attacks. Other doctors spread rumors that what I was doing was illegal—of course it wasn't—or that it was dangerous. Imagine someone saying riboflavin eye drops and ultraviolet light are more dangerous than a transplant procedure!"

I got the sense that no matter how often he told this story, the indignity still infuriated him. Profit wasn't the only motive, certainly. There was a lot of "not invented here" skepticism, just as there is with any breakthrough. Vigorous questioning and review are part of any process, especially in medicine where people's lives are on the line. But I also felt certain that Dr. Boxer Wachler wasn't entirely wrong. Threatening people's livelihoods, practices, and reputations can cause them to go dingbat crazy. I have no doubt that some doctors threw every roadblock they could in Dr. Boxer Wachler's path in order to protect themselves and their way of life.

"Everyone assumes that it must be glamorous being a pioneer," he said. "Truth is, most of the pioneers who got out of the covered wagons ended up with arrows in their backs."

That was a truth that transcended all professions. American bobsledders weren't supposed to contend in the World Cup, so when we started winning races, the Germans, Swiss, and Russians fired every arrow they could at us. There were rumors that we cheated, which was nonsense. Then there were rumors about our personal lives, which came with the territory. It happens everywhere. Billy Beane threatened the status quo in baseball and almost lost his job when he employed statistical modeling as general manager of the Oakland Athletics (a story captured in the book and movie *Moneyball*). Doctors are no different. It just infuriated me to think of all the people whose lives could have been changed in the four years that Dr. Boxer Wachler had spent pulling arrows out of his back.

"So we'll schedule you for tomorrow," he said. "The procedure takes only about thirty minutes. It's noninvasive. You'll want to rest your eyes immediately afterward, but you will feel no discomfort at all, and after that you'll be on your way."

"What if it doesn't work?" I asked, still reluctant to believe that a miracle of this magnitude could be as simple as vitamin B and light.

"If it doesn't work, you'll either have a transplant or lose your sight," he said. "But you're going blind anyway, so you really don't have much to lose."

It was hard to argue with that logic. But I couldn't allow myself to get too excited. Disappointment was just around the corner, I was sure of it. As wonderful and convincing as Dr. Boxer Wachler's presentation had been, it sounded far too holistic to be real. I felt certain that this was like those macrobiotic and herbal cancer treatments, where some patients claimed to be cured, but most don't make it.

I went back to my hotel room and enjoyed the rest of the day in the California sun, expecting nothing more than the warmth of the moment and the promise of the day. If this turned out to be real, my world would be changed forever. If not, I would press ahead one step at a time.

The procedure took almost no time. The following day, I showed up at Dr. Boxer Wachler's office expecting to be ushered into a surgical suite or at least prepped for a procedure. Instead, he had me sit in a La-Z-Boy and lean back while he put drops in my eye. There was no anesthesia, no incisions; the Lasik had been far more invasive. After the drops were in, he had me stare into a light. It didn't pulse or throw off any heat, but it was bright enough to get my attention. I lay in the recliner for thirty minutes, and when the light went out, Dr. Boxer Wachler said, "Okay, that's it."

"That's what?" I said.

"That's the procedure," he said. "We have some dark glasses for you to wear for a couple of days, at least until you come back, but that's the C3-R procedure."

I didn't feel any different when I left than when I came in. There was no healing sensation, no superhero moment where I felt my eyes become stronger. Before I got back to the hotel, I convinced myself that this had been a waste of time. You couldn't have watched one episode of *CSI: Miami* in the amount of time I'd spent in that office. To somehow assume that this was all it took to cure a disease that had threatened to take everything away from me was just plain foolish.

I slept well and even swam a little, something I'd never been able to do in December since I was always on the ice. Two days later I went back to Dr. Boxer Wachler's office for a follow-up. He was as jovial and upbeat as ever as he examined my eyes with various contraptions.

"Looks like we have a winner," he said.

"What do you mean?" I asked.

"You're all clear. The keratoconus has been arrested. You can go back to racing."

"Wha . . . What?" I mumbled.

He broke into a wide smile. I could tell that he'd gotten similar reactions before, but that didn't dampen the thrill. Delivering such good news had to be one of the greatest feelings in the world, although not nearly as fulfilling as knowing that you had given someone a reprieve from blindness.

"Your eyes are no longer degenerating," he said. "You're not any better than you were when you came, but you won't get any worse. The contacts you have now should get you through this season. Come back in the spring and we'll perform the second procedure, the one that'll get you seeing clearly again."

He said it so plainly that I could barely absorb what I was hearing. I had come to Beverly Hills because I had nowhere else to go. I had basically retired from my sport. I had fallen so deeply into despair that I had done the stupidest thing imaginable. And now, just like that, I was being told I was cured. My vision was still 20/1000 without lenses, and I would have to come back for another, more invasive procedure after the season to insert corrective lenses, but I had managed with my current level of vision for several months. It wasn't great—in fact, it was terrible—but it was a breeze as long as I knew that it wouldn't get any worse. For several minutes I couldn't wrap my head around what had just happened. The disease that was supposed to rob me of my dreams was gone. The downward spiral had stopped.

I was, for reasons I could never explain, the recipient of yet another miracle.

I tried to thank Dr. Boxer Wachler, but the words caught in my throat. Then I realized that he didn't need to hear my words. The tears said it all.

ELEVEN
The Beach

I came out of retirement almost as fast as I went in. One of my first calls from California was to Brian Shimer to let him know that I still couldn't see, but I wasn't getting worse. My vision was the same after my first procedure with Dr. Brian Boxer Wachler, as it has been when I won the World Cup, so if Brian and the team still wanted me, I was ready to race.

I owed Brian more than I could ever repay. He had forced me to come clean about my disease, and he hadn't walked away from me, even though he knew I hadn't at first been forthcoming with him. A lot of coaches would have dismissed me and moved on. Brian responded as a compassionate human being and friend. Then he went above and beyond the call of duty by bringing in Scott Stoll, who found Dr. Boxer Wachler.

Brian had also gone to bat for me with the USOC and the USA Bobsled and Skeleton Federation. Dr. Boxer Wachler's second procedure—the one to add the lenses—wasn't cheap, even though he worked very closely with me to cut the best deal possible. No matter how big a discount he gave me, I still couldn't have paid for it on my own. Despite my recent success on the World Cup circuit, bobsledding didn't pay any more now than it did before. But Brian stepped in and persuaded the bobsled federation and USOC officials to foot the bills for my procedure, even though he knew there was a good chance it wouldn't work, meaning I would still be out of the sport. He didn't do it as a coach; he did it as a humanitarian. By getting them to pay, Brian provided yet another miracle in what was becoming a growing network of humbling events.

With the knowledge that my eyesight would not get worse, I couldn't wait to get back in the sled. I drove the remainder of the 2007–2008 season with an invigorated spirit and a renewed sense of purpose. To my surprise, my teammates weren't bitter, even though they had every right to be furious with me for what I'd done. Their lives had been in my hands, and not only could I not see, I wasn't making the greatest decisions. If I had been in their shoes, I would have been upset at me. But they handled my return just as they handled my departure: like true professionals who wanted nothing more than what was best for me and for the team. They must have believed that I gave the team the best chance at success, because they seemed genuinely excited to see me.

Our finishes weren't as great as they had been in 2006–2007, but our attitude and optimism were better than ever. I still couldn't see my hands in front of my face without contacts, but my lenses were not becoming obsolete since my vision had stabilized, and I wasn't carrying a soul-zapping secret. Everyone knew about my procedure and my prognosis, and everyone in U.S. bobsledding felt a sense of renewal.

Some of what I'd gone through would remain private, but I also felt compelled to tell my story as often as possible. I had no idea how many people were struggling with keratoconus as I had, but I knew that Dr. Boxer Wachler wasn't famous enough. Imagine if someone discovered a cure for diabetes that involved light and vitamins and nobody knew about it. That was the equivalent of what I had discovered through Dr. Boxer Wachler. He had turned a devastating disease into an annoyance, like a wart or an ingrown toenail. Yet the general population remained painfully unaware that this miraculous treatment existed. It became my mission to get the word out.

—◦—

In March 2008, right after the final race of the World Cup season, I returned to Beverly Hills for procedure number two. Again Dr. Boxer Wachler greeted me in his office like an old friend. "I want to take you out to dinner," he said right off the bat.

I had never had an ophthalmologist take me out to eat, but I'd never been cured of blindness before either. He picked me up from my hotel in a 1971 Dodge Charger, perfectly restored, with a 440 engine that rumbled like a prowling lion.

"I have twin girls, very young; my wife and I got started late," he said, noting how family responsibilities have cut into his time for rowing. "But I still find time to work on my passion, which is restoring old muscle cars." He's had Ford Mustangs and Chevrolet Chevelles, a 1967 Plymouth Belvedere (one of the more underappreciated muscle cars), and a 1970 Plymouth Road Runner with a 426 Hemi and retractable hood scoop, as well as the greatest muscle car of all time, the Pontiac GTO.

After talking about cars, we turned to racing and training and the mental rigors of having an extended career as an athlete. Most people who play sports in school have a short window—four, maybe eight years at most—when they are competitive. After that they might play recreationally or in various leagues, but their intense days are behind them. Professional and Olympic athletes have to keep that level of competitive intensity for years, sometimes decades. The physical toll is well chronicled, but the mental strain that comes with staying on top of your game season after season is less evident. We chatted about that and other topics.

He took me to Mastro's Steakhouse in Beverly Hills, where we ate like kings and talked about family and friends. Dr.

Boxer Wachler told me about some of the more interesting celebrities he's treated. I shared tales of growing up in Park City and some of the funnier stories of my first forays overseas. "We were at this one spa, and I'm relaxing in a steam room when this completely naked middle-aged couple comes in and sits down next to me," I said. "Thankfully they didn't speak English and I didn't speak German. I mean, what's your first line in that situation? 'Nice to see you?'"

When he dropped me back off at the hotel, he said, "The procedure in the morning will take no more than half an hour. It's about ten minutes per eye. After a day or two of rest, you should be as good as new."

It was hard for me to believe that it could be that easy, but I hadn't believed that riboflavin and ultraviolet light could keep me from going completely blind either.

The next morning when I arrived at the office, Dr. Boxer Wachler went into a little more detail. This procedure was called Visian ICL. ICL stands for "implantable collamer lens," which was, as the name implied, a lens that would be surgically implanted behind the iris of each eye, like an internal permanent contact.

"You'll be fully conscious," he said. "I'll put numbing drops in each eye so there will no pain at all. Then I'll make a small incision behind the iris and insert the lens. That's it. You should be ready to go home in no time."

Of course, I had to take my existing contacts out before going into the operating area, which left me so blind that I couldn't see my own feet. A nurse had to lead me to the chair by the arm. Once I was seated, Dr. Boxer Wachler said, "Can you see that painting on the wall in front of you?"

"What wall?" I said.

He chuckled and said, "Lean back. This will take only a few minutes."

A lot of people get so squeamish at the thought of having anything in or near their eyes—or just hearing about it—that I have be careful when I talk about Dr. Boxer Wachler's procedures. Granted, having a lens inserted behind your iris isn't like having a boil lanced, but once you get past the anxiety, the procedure itself is a breeze. The numbing drops worked perfectly, and the whole thing took less time than a lot of eye exams I had taken; it was definitely much less intrusive than the Lasik had been.

Twenty minutes after lying down, fully conscious, I sat up.

Of course, there was a chance that the procedure wouldn't work. Corrective lens insertion is risky. If I had more deterioration than anticipated, the lenses might prove ineffective. My sight wouldn't be worse, but it probably wouldn't be better.

Dr. Boxer Wachler was anxious to see if it had been effective. "Now do you see the painting?" he asked.

I looked at the wall I hadn't been able to see earlier and saw a watercolor landscape of a beach, one of the first projects assigned to an intermediate art student, not a masterpiece by any means. I felt sure it was a gift from a friend or family member, something painted on a Saturday morning in Malibu. But to me, it was the most beautiful painting I'd ever seen.

Not only could I see the painting, but I could see the patterns in the wallpaper and I could count the drawers in a cabinet ten feet away. I could see books and magazines on the counter, and the intricate carvings of the antique Asian sculpture on the sideboard in the outer office. Because it had been so long since I'd had perfect eyesight, I'd forgotten how clear the world could be. I could see the crow's feet around Dr. Boxer Wachler's eyes as he smiled and the small cracks in the tile floor. I could also read the eye chart and throw a tissue into the trash can more than five feet away. I could read Dr. Boxer Wachler's framed diplomas and see the fine print on the brochures.

My eyes were not bandaged for weeks like you see in the movies. Shapes didn't form slowly as I adjusted to my new-found sight. When I first sat down in Dr. Boxer Wachler's chair, I couldn't see the wall in front of me. When I got up, I could see the world. My cure was as instantaneous as scales falling from my eyes. I was blind, but now I could see.

TWELVE
The Night Train

hen I walked out of Dr. Brian Boxer Wachler's office, I composed a long email on my phone that started out dire and morose, as if I were saying good-bye to everyone. "I know you all are thinking about me and I want to thank you all for standing by and supporting me . . ." Then, about ten lines in, I wrote, "Ha! Got you suckers! I can see better than all of you. Get ready. Holcomb's back."

Within seconds Brian Shimer shot a note back that said, "Don't ever do anything like that again. You scared me to death. Welcome back to the light. Now get to work. We've got a World Championship to win."

I did exactly that, heading back to the Olympic Training Center in Colorado Springs for a summer training session that was as intense and fulfilling as any I'd ever been through. Part of what made it so great was my renewed spirit. It's a lot easier to hit the weight room with a focused mind when you don't have a distraction like blindness hanging over you. Throughout the spring and summer, I lifted harder than ever, ran faster than I thought possible, and pushed myself every minute of the day. I ran the "Incline," an old cog railroad trail that runs up the side of Pike's Peak, to build my endurance, increasing my speed when my legs began to burn. The sweat burning in my eyes was a sweet reminder that I had been given a second chance, a new lease on life. Not a second could be wasted. Every opportunity had to be seized.

I worked on plyometric exercises to improve my explosiveness, and I expanded my fast-twitch drills to keep my reflexes sharp. Every morning I would work out hard for three hours, take a break, and then hit it again in the afternoon. There were times—infrequent and short-lived—when the demon tried to intrude (depression, as it turns out, isn't as quickly cured as keratoconus), but I found that nothing improves your outlook more than physical exertion. The harder I worked, the happier I became.

And why wouldn't I be happy? For the first time in my life, I would be racing with 20/20 vision without contact lenses. I had no idea how that would feel, but I figured it had to be better than driving blind. Unfortunately, it wasn't long before I encountered a problem I never saw coming.

The World Championships were going to be held in Lake Placid in late February and early March of 2009. This gave my team a tremendous advantage. We would be competing on the track we knew better than any other, the one we trained on every year, and we'd be accustomed to the Eastern time zone already as well. An extra bonus was that we'd be able to order pizza in English and buy a Coke in a vending machine with a dollar—things that didn't happen very often in World Championship competition. My teammates and I had all this in mind when we headed to Lake Placid to train in the fall of 2008.

But in the first few weeks of training, I realized that something wasn't right. During my early runs, I saw trees and flagpoles and chunks of ice dancing like white birds on the wind. I saw the shimmer of the track and faint imprints from previous runs. I saw clouds overhead and people standing near the edge of the track. And my head hurt. When a piece of debris flew off the sled during one of my runs, I ducked and said, "Whoa, what was that?" It was dirt or ice or maybe a small bit of Fiberglass from the sled, nothing unusual. Small bits of debris whizzed by our heads all the time. The problem was I'd never seen it before.

I was seeing as well as anybody on the track, which proved to be a problem. My sight was too good. Because I had been driving blind for so long, my style was to feel my way down the track without any visual cues. Now that I could see everything, my brain was fighting over which senses should dominate during a run. I felt like my head was going to explode from all the stimuli.

183

I never thought I would see too well, but as I looked at some of the anemic times we were posting in practice, that was clearly the case.

I went to Brian right away when I realized what was happening. I had learned. No more secrets.

"What are you going to do about it?" he asked.

I looked at my helmet after a day of practice runs. The visor was fogged over from the change in temperature. As it thawed out, it left a thin layer of dust and dirt that was in the air. Any other time I would have cleaned it right away, if not replaced my visor completely. Most drivers obsess about keeping their visors clean, some going so far as to replace their visor every day whether it's scratched or not.

"I'm not going to clean that up," I said, pointing to the dirt that had accumulated on the helmet and the scratches and fog on the visor.

Brian's head went back in surprise. "Really?" he said.

"My problem is I'm seeing too well," I said. "I don't want to be totally blind again, but hey, given where I've come from a little dirt should make the world just fuzzy enough."

I got a lot of funny looks the next day. My helmet looked like it had come out of a monster truck rally, and the other guys couldn't believe that I wasn't going to clean it. At the top level of any sport, athletes do all sorts of little things to mess around with their opponents. After the Dallas Mavericks won the conference title in 2011, the team's then shooting guard Jason Terry had the NBA Championship trophy tattooed on the inside of his right bicep so that whenever he went up for a jump shot, the guy guarding him could see the trophy perched behind the ball. It was brash, but it also threw a lot of defenders off their game.

Reggie White, the Pro Football Hall of Fame defensive end for the Green Bay Packers, used to sing hymns as he lined up. After some of his more vicious sacks, he would pat the quarterback on the helmet and say, "Jesus loves you." Reggie was an ordained minister, so he meant it, but he also knew that his messages threw the other team off-kilter. My dirty helmet and scratched visor did the same thing to my competitors. In a sport where drivers took their helmets to bed with them at night (not really, but close), letting grit build up gave me an air and an edge. I didn't realize it at the time, but that was just one of the many ways we would intimidate the competition throughout the year.

In addition to the World Championships being on our home soil, one of the main reasons we felt so confident going into the 2008–2009 season was the quality of our equipment. Bo-Dyn Bobsleds kept getting better every year. Geoff Bodine's relentless pursuit of continuous improvement and his obsession with cutting-edge engineering had not just rescued American bobsledding—he had revolutionized the sport. In the eighteen years since Geoff brought his NASCAR philosophy to bobsled racing, American teams had gone from buying second-rate sleds from the Europeans to being the envy of the bobsledding world. In the fall of 2008, Geoff and his designers upped the game again.

It was October, early enough in the World Cup season that

everyone was still getting their competitive wits about them but far enough along that the pecking order was beginning to take shape. The top contenders included us, the Germans (as usual), led by Andre "The Cannibal" Lange, along with the Russians, the Swiss, and a surprisingly good team from Latvia with an ambitious driver named Janis Minins. Andre and I were perhaps the two best drivers in the world at the time, but any one of half a dozen teams could win any given event. There was no room for error.

We had left Lake Placid and had arrived in Park City, Utah, for the 2008 National Team Trials. I had a bye on to the team for my previous year's results, so I had to compete in trials, but it didn't really matter how I did. Given that, the Bo-Dyn engineers took the opportunity to break out a new sled they had designed specifically for the Vancouver Olympics. The best way to test a sled, of course, is to race it.

Now, this sled was a rather unusual one.

It wasn't uncommon for new sleds to show up unpainted and put together just well enough to test out. Typically they would throw a coating of gray primer on to clean it up a bit, but not spend the money on a full paint job. This time, they changed it up: it was a black primer and the sled looked like it was built for Batman. In fact, we called it The Dark Knight, after the movie that was just released.

On the first run, I knew this was something special. The lines were perfect, and it felt like a rocket going down the track. The entry into the turns was clean and it handled beautifully. We had very little jostling on the exits and minimal vibration through the transitions. It also looked fast: flat black with a kind of old-school muscle car coolness that made you think of Steve McQueen or Evel Knievel. When we got out, the engineers from Bo-Dyn were waiting.

"We'll take it," I said.

Their eyes got wide and they looked at each other. "I don't know," one of the engineers said. "We're just supposed to try this out. I don't know if it's ready yet. It's a prototype."

"Ready?" I asked, incredulously. "It's the fastest sled on the track. You've got to let us race it."

After some emergency phone calls, the engineering crew came back and said, "Okay, let us take it back to the shop."

Another round of calls ensued, this one discussing how quickly (or not) we could get the sled painted. I could see the conversations getting quite animated. I didn't think it would come to it, but if there was any more pushback, I was prepared to call Geoff myself. I would have to say only one word to him: Earnhardt. Geoff had raced enough against Dale Earnhardt Sr. to know that part of his reputation as "The Intimidator" came from his flat black No. 3 race car. According to drivers who raced in that era, you only had to be bounced off the track one or two times before you started checking your mirror for that black Chevy. This sled had the same look, and I was determined to race it exactly the way it was. Thankfully, I didn't have to get Geoff involved. One of the engineers looked at me with the phone to his ear and gave a thumbs-up.

–◦–

After the National Team Trials, we had to part ways temporarily with our new sled. The new sled went to Connecticut to get painted while we left Park City for Whistler, British Columbia, thirty miles north of Vancouver. Here we got our first look at the 2010 Olympic sliding track. It was a beast of a track, very fast and very dangerous. The only way to get around it was to attack it, which is what we did.

It wasn't always smooth sailing. During that week in late October, every country was given the opportunity to take ten runs down the track at Whistler for the first time. Days one and two were all two-man runs. Day three was a different story: eight teams had decided to give four-man a try. Of those eight sleds, four ended up crashing in the same spot, curve thirteen, the second of four turns in the labyrinth that track officials were calling the Gold Rush Trail, because gold could be won or lost there.

That evening, after training, we got word that the Whistler Track crew was going to reshape the ice in curve thirteen to ensure that the sleds would be able to make it down successfully. Hearing the news, we decided that we were going to pull the four-man sled out and give it a shot. I was confident in my three days of two-man training and didn't have too many reservations about it, until we saw the start list. We were going to be the first sled off the hill the next day. I hesitantly joked saying, "Well, we have a fifty-fifty chance of getting through curve thirteen."

Later that night, after finishing some Chinese food, the guys ripped open one of the brown bags and wrote "Curve 50-50" on it. The next morning, as we inspected the track like we do before every training session, I stood at the exit of curve thirteen and taped it to the wooden lip of the curve. Everybody but the president of the International Bobsled & Skeleton Federation, who happened to be Canadian, thought it was very fitting. It didn't take long for him to express his feelings and tear down the sign, but the name stuck. (By the time the first race came in late February, with us all back in Vancouver during the World Cup competitions, all the television announcers referred to curve thirteen as "Curve 50-50.")

After a week of training in Whistler, it was time to cross the pond to begin the World Cup Circuit.

—◄○►—

When we reached Europe, we were reunited with the sleek new sled we'd raced in Park City. We pulled it out of the box, excited to see what kind of paint job they came up with on such short notice. We were all floored when there was no paint job at all. They simply covered the primer with a sticker. We were all taken aback, and nobody said a word. Finally, after a few seconds, someone said, "The Night Train? What the hell is The Night Train?"

We instantly went to the phones. After a few minutes, we got the official word. They didn't have time to paint it, and since we were so bent on having it for the season, they just slapped "The Night Train" stickers on and shipped it out.

The next week and the week after, we would pull the sled out of the shipping crate and hear people at the track say, "Look, it's The Night Train." Very few fans recognized us, but everyone knew the sled. It was the only bobsled at any race that wasn't shiny and ornate. And it was the only one everyone knew by name.

I loved it. Our guys began playing up the badass image that went with driving a sled that looked like the Ford Mustang in *Bullitt*. We didn't say much and didn't acknowledge the oohs and ahs as we were carrying the sled to the starting line. We even got new flat black uniforms and helmets.

Some of the engineers fretted about it not being shiny.

"Tell them it's a special paint from NASA," I said jokingly.

Somebody did just that, and before Thanksgiving a rumor circulated that Bo-Dyn was in league with NASA to develop secret space paint for bobsleds. I had to bite my lip whenever I heard that one. I would have never believed that black primer could generate so much buzz.

The sled and the uniforms and my decision to let dirt and scratches build up on my visor, which was just enough to skew my vision the needed amount, all combined to give us a look of invincibility, like Clint Eastwood riding into town, dusty and unshaven, with a cigarillo between his teeth. Of course, all of those things would have been comical if we had finished in the middle of the pack. But we were putting together some of the best results in the history of American bobsledding.

A few months later, at the end of a sensational World Cup Circuit, we found ourselves back in my hometown. On the Park City sliding track, in the final event before the World Championships, we put together a clean sweep, leading after every heat and winning two gold medals. That win and the great runs we'd had throughout the season gave us a bronze medal in the 2009 World Cup overall standings. It also made us one of the favorites going into Lake Placid, even though no American had won the bobsled World Championships in fifty years.

The pressure couldn't have been greater, but I didn't feel nervous. If anything, I felt a sense of exhilaration and relief. A year and a half ago, I had been legally blind and lost in a sea of despair. But now I could see, not just with my eyes but with my heart and soul. I had been rescued from the abyss for this moment. Now I had to make it count.

-◄○►-

World Championships are the biggest non-Olympic events in our sport, with all the pressure of the Olympic Games but without as much fanfare and outside distractions. Fans came out to Lake Placid in full force. I couldn't imagine where they'd come from or where they were staying. Lake Placid is a little place that's not on the way to anywhere. Every year during training I looked around and marveled that the Olympics had been held here in 1980. Accommodations and hospitality were scarce, but sports fans somehow found a way to turn out in the thousands. From February 20 to March 1, 2009, nothing in the area was placid.

The two-man competition took place on February 21 and 22. My pusher for five years was Curt Tomasevicz, my

Cornhusker buddy who had been an academic All-American football player at Nebraska before joining me in the sled. Since the story of my miraculous cure from keratoconus was slowly getting out, Curt agreed to an interview with *USA Today*. At the time, he told the reporter, "I took my first trip in October of 2004, and Steve was my driver. Before we went down, he was just dousing his eyes with contact solution. It made me nervous. But after five years, I know that I wouldn't rather be behind any other driver."

Those words touched me deeply, but I couldn't get caught up in the emotions. Curt and I had work to do.

Andre Lange of Germany was the defending champion and the man everyone thought would take the two-man title again. A methodical, unemotional assassin, Andre was the prototypical German bobsled athlete: precise and all business. Off the track he was a friendly guy who would buy you a beer and tell you a joke. But during competition, he was a robo-driver.

It was not a surprise that Germany had the fastest first run. What was shocking was that it wasn't Andre. Thomas Florschütz and his pusher Marc Kühn had a near-flawless first run to take the lead. The Swiss team, Ivo Rüegg and Cedric Grand, was a close second, and Curt and I were a solid third. Andre was in fifth, an uncharacteristic struggle for a man who had won the World Championships three times.

The lead swapped after the second run, with the Swiss taking the lead and Florschütz and Kühn dropping to second. We remained third and appeared to have bronze locked up. It was unlikely we could improve our position unless something crazy happened with Rüegg and Grand. Curt and I blocked out what everyone else was doing and focused on making our final runs. When the snow settled, we had taken the bronze behind Switzerland and Germany. It was a solid finish. But we all hoped for much better in The Night Train.

The four-man was the final event of the week, February 28 and March 1. It's officially called the Mt. Van Hoevenberg Olympic Bobsled Run even though it's located closer to Hurricane Mountain, nestled in the middle of the woods in a spot on the U.S. National Register of Historical Places. It's also the only sliding track in the world with a turn named after a NASCAR driver. Turn nineteen, the penultimate curve, is called Trickle, named for Wisconsin native Dick Trickle because he crashed a bobsled there in 2006 in the Bodine Bobsled Challenge, an annual event Geoff hosts to cross-promote NASCAR and bobsledding. By the time we got to Trickle, after navigating turns five through nine (known as the Devil's Highway) and Benham's Bend (turn fourteen), our fate and finish would be sealed.

An almost eerie calm nestled over me as we stood at the starting line for our first run. Not only had I visualized these runs thousands of times in my mind, but I had driven on this track enough times that I could do it, well, blind.

We got off to a fantastic start, and I could sense that the rest of the team—Curt, Steve Mesler, and Justin Olsen—felt as calm and confident as I did. When we crossed the finish line after the first run, I looked up and saw that we were in first.

The second was a mirror image of the first. Once again

we were in the lead, posting the best times in each of the first two runs.

Normally, nothing is harder than sleeping on a lead, but I fell into the sleep of the dead after day one. It surprised me how peaceful I felt. This was the biggest moment of my career, and the biggest moment for U.S. bobsledding in half a century. Yet I felt a serenity that was as calm as the snow-fed waters of the lake. There was no doubt that winning the World Championships would forever alter my life, but nothing could compare to the way I had already been changed. I wanted to win, sure. In fact, I felt confident that we would win. But I also understood that these bobsled runs had a greater meaning and that my life had a larger purpose than the medals or trophies I won. I wasn't supposed to be in that position at all. I had tried to kill myself and my vision had almost taken me out of the game permanently. Yet here I was, going for the World Championship title and then for an Olympic gold medal. And when it would all be over, my bigger purpose would just be beginning: I had a story to tell. It is one about hope, perseverance, and overcoming adversity. And I would let the world know how the C3-R procedure can stop the progressing blindness of keratoconus.

—◦—

Day two drew the largest crowds. It was the last day of the championships and everyone came out to see the grand finale. We also attracted novices who wouldn't know a bobsled runner from a boomerang, because everyone wanted to say they had witnessed the first American World Championship title since 1959.

"Two runs to make history," I said to the team. The words weren't necessary. I could tell from the looks in their eyes that they were ready to break the American drought.

Our third run was once again the best of the day and put the gold almost completely out of reach for Andre and his team, who had been nipping at our heels in second place throughout. All I had to do was avoid any terrible mistakes on the final run and we would win the title.

We loaded and hit the first time mark in 5.10 seconds, a great start given what we needed. Through turn three our total time was 3:02.29, a 0.73 second lead over the Germans with the Devil's Highway still to come.

We hit it perfectly, taking each turn high and coming out smooth, no chatter or hard hits. By the time we hit Chicane (turns fifteen and sixteen) it was over. Our lead was 0.92 seconds. The only remaining question was if we would post the best time in each of the four heats.

When we crossed the finish line I glanced up and saw the "1" by USA-1. I was overwhelmed. A second later I saw that our time was 54.30 seconds, the fastest of the heat, for a total of 3:36.61. We had blown away the field by almost a full second and made history for American bobsledding. The crowd was cheering like it was the Super Bowl.

Germany finished second, and Latvia took third, the first medal by that country in World Championship history.

Andre was one of the first to congratulate us, not a blow-by handshake but a heartfelt gesture with a big smile on his face. In reviewing the tape of the race later, I saw that Andre was one of the first to jump to his feet in applause after we passed through Chicane and it was obvious that we had won. His nickname might be "The Cannibal," but Andre is a class act. He was also a fierce competitor. I knew he would be gunning for us in the 2010 Olympic Games.

We hoisted the World Championship trophy in Lake Placid almost a year to the day after the second procedure to restore my sight. At the time I hadn't reflected on all the things that had come together in order for me to be standing on the podium with my teammates: the training, the teamwork, the commitment of men like Brian Shimer, who had laid the foundation for bobsledding in America, and the advancements in equipment thanks to Geoff Bodine. Then there was the medical miracle by Dr. Brian Boxer Wachler and the never-say-never attitude of men like Scott Stoll. Without any one of those components, we probably would have failed. But because all the right forces came together at exactly the right moment, we were able to make history and go into the Olympic Games in Vancouver as the favorites for gold: another first for Americans in our sport.

Epilogue

E ven though Andre Lange was the consummate gentleman, German sports fans were not at all pleased to lose the World Championship. The Germans and Swiss consider bobsledding World Championships to be a two-country event, the birthright of the Alpine nations. Sliding on ice is in the Germanic DNA. They look at bobsledding the way Americans look at baseball. It's their game; they should win it.

Germans who followed the sport closely could justify losing to us at Lake Placid. That was, after all, our home track. But Vancouver in the 2010 Olympics was a neutral site, and Germany had won gold in the previous four Olympic Games. Going back to 1976, the country had taken gold in seven of the last nine Winter Olympics, the kind of run the Soviets once had in hockey. Three of the four members of the Germany-1 sled had gold medals back home from the 2002 and 2006 Games. Andre was the guy who beat Todd Hays and Brian Shimer in the Salt Lake City Olympics. They were a potent force—and we were in their sights from the beginning.

I was so happy to have had experience in Torino. It was one thing to go to the Games as a rookie Olympian with no expectations. It was another to be World Champions and the gold-medal favorite. Having already stayed in an Olympic village, gone through the hoopla of an opening ceremony, seen the enormity of the press coverage, and experienced the distractions of everything going on around, I knew what to expect in Canada, which was a huge advantage.

My family traveled to Whistler for the Games, as did Geoff Bodine and Dr. Brian Boxer Wachler. I'm sure they went through the same orientation ("Your child/friend is here to compete, not entertain you. Please don't expect to see them much before their event."), but by this time everyone except Dr. Boxer Wachler was a veteran; he had plenty of people around to steer him in the right direction.

The story of my miraculous comeback from blindness and the cure that saved my career (and perhaps my life) was all over the news. NBC did one of its famous "profile" segments on my keratoconus, as did ESPN and more foreign networks than I could count. I felt fortunate to be able to tell my story to the world and hopefully help others who were suffering from the disease that almost robbed me of everything. I had to manage my time, but I also knew that I had an obligation to get the word out.

Of course, winning would help that cause considerably.

Bobsledding was one of the final events of the Olympics, with the two-man competition beginning on February 20, eight days after the Opening Ceremony. The four-man was held on February 26 and 27, finishing less than twenty-four hours before the Closing Ceremony. We had plenty of time to talk to the media and see other events, but we also had a lot of time to think about the enormity of what lay ahead.

Most athletes don't feel pressure when they are in the midst of competition. During a run, my teammates and I don't feel nervous at all. It's the run-up that gets you. Anxiety is the evil stepsister of anticipation. The longer you wait, the more gremlins creep into your psyche. Like everyone, we had a great time at the Opening Ceremony, but after that we tried to block everything out and focus on our practice. Thankfully, Whistler Sliding Centre was seventy-eight miles north of Vancouver at the base of serene Blackcomb Mountain, which gave us some room away from the craziness.

The track was anything but serene. Not only had an athlete been killed just hours before the opening ceremony, but crashes were happening almost every day. There was little doubt that this was the most dangerous track ever to host a major competition. When Georgian luger Nodar Kumaritashvili flew off the track, he was reportedly going eighty-nine miles an hour. Because of that fatal incident, the starting lines for the men's and women's luge competitions were moved. The men started at what was originally intended to be the women's starting house and women started in the junior house. The bobsled starting line stayed the same, but everyone was on edge.

Curt and I competed in the two-man competition on February 20 and 21, and after the first run, we knew we were looking at an uphill battle. Despite the second-fastest start time, we were fifth at the end of the opening heat with a time of 51.89 seconds, three-tenths behind Andre and his pusher, Kevin Kuske. It got no better after that. Our second run was 52.04 seconds, while Andre got in with 51.72 to take a commanding lead. We hovered around our same times on day two, never beating Andre. At the end, our total time was 3:27.94, good enough for sixth, but a full 1.29 seconds behind the Germans, who took gold easily.

Germany won gold and silver in the two-man, with Thomas Florschütz and Richard Adjei coming in second, 0.22 seconds behind their countrymen. Russia won bronze, edging out Switzerland by three-tenths of a second for the final spot on the medal stand.

Curt and I were disappointed, but we didn't think about it long. Our teammates and The Night Train were waiting.

The four-man competition started on a Friday, with two heats the first day and two the second. The start order was set by World Cup ranking. Winning the four-man World Cup title, we were given the number-one draw. We broke the start record by one-hundredth of a second. With that fast start and nearly flawless drive, we set a track record of 50.89.

My teammate Justin Olsen slapped my shoulders as we were getting out. We had gotten through Curve 50-50 without so much as a wiggle, and our times through the remaining three curves were not just the best in the field but the best time ever recorded on the track.

Andre and his team were up next, and they put down an even faster start of 4.73 seconds, breaking the track record we just set. But he didn't didn't take advantage of that fast start and finished with a 51.14.

Our second run was even faster. We broke our own record by three-hundredths of a second, finishing in 50.86. At the end of the day, we led the Germans by just over four-tenths of a second, the equivalent of two quick eye blinks or eight flaps of a hummingbird's wings.

Back-to-back days of racing are difficult. After day one, I wanted to lay low and relax so I'd be fully recovered for the next day. I sent texts and emails to my family and Dr. Boxer Wachler, and everyone wished me good luck. That made me smile. Luck had nothing to do with it. I felt confident about the runs, but I also understood that this was our time and we were in the position for reasons that transcended luck or fortune or even our own individual efforts. There was a destiny to this moment. I might have been the only one to understand it at that moment, but I believed it deep in my soul. No American had won a gold medal in bobsledding since 1948, so Saturday was going to be a big day and a big deal.

Late Friday night I lay in my bed and visualized the runs over and over. My head moved up at the apex of the turns (when you're at a ninety-degree angle through a turn you look up to see where you're going instead of left or right), and my hands moved as I pulled the rings. I tried to feel the sled against my feet and knees and the small seat around my hips. I imagined my teammates crowding in behind me and the cold wind riding over my helmet like a wave.

On Saturday afternoon, Brian Shimer gave us some encouraging words, but more than anything I remember him asking how I slept. "I slept great," I said. "I always do, at least now." That was truer than anyone knew. My focus was sharp and my desire intense, but I wasn't losing sleep over anything anymore.

Our third run was slightly slower than the track records we had set the day before but still good enough to be the fastest of the day. We got off to a 4.77-second start, which was conservative but only two-hundredths of a second slower than our first run and four-hundredths slower than our record-setting time on Friday afternoon. We made it down in 51.19 seconds, extending our lead to a half second—a mile in a sled on a sheet of ice with sixteen turns and we led by less than one dribble of a basketball.

That set up a finale for the ages. Andre wanted to win this gold medal worse than any in his life, in part because he was behind but also because he had come into this Olympics as the underdog for the first time. That added a layer of motivation to his already hypercompetitive nature. A solid run by Andre in the fourth heat would put the pressure on us. I knew that was what he was thinking. And I knew we wouldn't succumb.

—◦—

The final heat goes out in reverse order from last to first. The Night Train would be the final sled on the ice in this Olympic Games, and we would go out right behind Canada-1.

Andre showed no emotion. He patted his teammates on the shoulders and windmilled his arms to loosen his rotator cuffs like a boxer about to enter the ring.

Once in position, Andre nodded his head slightly and the Germans took off. They pushed the sled perfectly, hitting the first time mark in 4.74 seconds, the exact same time they had posted in their third run an hour earlier. It was a testament to German precision. Andre drove flawlessly as well. Each mark showed the Germans getting faster. When he made it cleanly through Curve 50-50, I knew he was having at a great run.

The time went on the board: 51.36, a great time. Germany-1's total was 3:24.84.

Then came Canada-1, a team that had taken advantage of the extra practice they had gotten from Canada's "Own the Podium" initiative. Lyndon Rush, a fine Canadian driver, put together a 51.46 time, not quite good enough to stay ahead of the Germans but good enough for a medal. The only remaining question was: Would it be silver or bronze?

We needed a solid time under 51.80 in this run to win. Our track record was 50.86. To win gold, we could not be one second slower than the fastest time ever run at the Whistler Sliding Centre.

Before the final heat began, I gathered our guys together and said, "This is it. It's now. This is our time."

My parents and sisters were too excited to engage in any

mental exercises. They bounced on their toes and screamed, "Go, Steven!" as loud as they could, even though they knew I couldn't hear them.

⤙○⤚

I start our run by taking off first. I could feel my teammates right behind me. We hit the sled perfectly, pushing it fast and loading without incident. Getting four large men in a small tube that is moving is no small feat no matter how often you do it. Our start time was 4.76—good, but two-hundredths slower than the Germans.

That wasn't a concern. We always seemed to start slower, but my guys loaded so cleanly and efficiently that we made it up before we got through the first turn. At the next split we were in the lead and looking good. All I had to do was get us through the Gold Rush Trail and Curve 50-50 without any major hiccups and we were home free.

My breathing was calm and my heart rate was as steady as it had been all week. The run progressed just as it had in my bed the night before, each turn coming like the downbeat of a song. When we hit Curve 50-50, I felt a stillness overcome me, and I knew that this was, indeed, our time. There aren't a lot of things we can control in life, but on the ice, in this turn, I knew I had control over the next few seconds. I controlled our destiny. And it was right here.

We got through the turn cleanly, exiting thirteen and entering fourteen with no bobbles and nothing slowing us down.

The two final turns were routine. When we came out of the last one and crossed the finish line, I knew we had won. I knew we had made history. And I knew that everything that I had been through—the struggles, the doubt, the hurt, the joy, and the miracles—had all been leading to this moment.

We were Olympic champions, the first American bobsledders to make that claim since Harry Truman was president and nobody in America owned a television.

My arms raised, and I heard the roars of the crowd and the shouts of my teammates. Justin Olsen has the voice of a lion. He let loose with the loudest "YEAH!" I'd ever heard. As we approached the finish area, all I could see was Brian leaning into the track with the number one held up and the biggest smile I had ever seen on his face. When we finally came to a stop, I was swallowed up in hugs and cheers and a sea of red, white, and blue.

Brian joined the celebration, grabbing all of us and yelling at the top of his lungs. I was still sitting in the sled, trying to get out, when Brian grabbed me. I thought he was going to rip my head off he was so excited. I had never seen Brian get that emotional, but he broke down after our win. A quarter century of commitment to the sport had finally paid off. He had been the foundation, the shoulders on which we stood. This was his moment as well.

Geoff Bodine wrapped me in a bear hug. I can't imagine him being any more excited when he won the Daytona 500. This was vindication for him: proof that getting into bobsledding was not a crazy sideshow idea.

I didn't see Dr. Boxer Wachler right away. But as I stood on the podium, the snow-capped mountains in the background, I knew that I was seeing those things because of him. That's when a warm, welcome mist filled my eyes, and for a brief moment, my vision blurred once more.

—◦—

Prior to the Vancouver Olympics I was one of the most anonymous people in America. No one outside my family and friends recognized me anywhere. That changed after we won gold. David Letterman asked me to come on and do a Top 10 List, and I've made countless appearances since. I speak to groups of all sizes and makeups.

But the impact of winning Olympic gold is much larger than going on late-night television or giving morning show interviews. I'm most proud of the moments that come in a Naples, Florida, pizzeria when Brian strolls in with his family to get dinner. The owner wipes his hands on a towel and tells the other customers, "Hey, you're not going to believe this, but that guy is the U.S. Olympic bobsled coach." There is the obligatory "You don't say," or "How 'bout that," but then another inevitable thing happens: a man approaches Brian and says, "I know you. I've had C3-R. It's a miracle. I can see again."

I visited the schools of my niece and my nephews after the Olympics. As I passed the gold medal around and let all the kids hold it and wear it, one of them said, "Weren't you blind?" When I responded, "Yes, I was, but I had a new procedure that fixed my eyes," the child came back with, "But now you see."

Indeed I do. Moments like that mean more than all the Olympic medals in the world.

A couple of weeks after winning gold in Vancouver, Dr. Boxer Wachler and I appeared on *The Doctors*, a syndicated show that informs the public about the latest medical breakthroughs. It was during that show that Dr. Boxer Wachler announced he was renaming the procedure Holcomb C3-R.

"There is only one other medical procedure named after an athlete: Tommy John surgery," he said. "This will be the first time in history that a procedure is named after an Olympian."

I choked out a "Thank you."

"No," he said. "Thank you. Because of you, people will know that there's hope, that their worlds don't have to be dark anymore."

For years I thought I was meant to win an Olympic gold medal, that I had been blessed with physical gifts and a competitive focus for that one, singular purpose. But that was never my destiny. Now I know that I am here to spread a message of hope.

Never give up and never let the demon inside overwhelm you. I was blind, but now I see.

Acknowledgments

Rising to meet challenges is what the Olympic spirit is all about. But I had no idea how many challenges would be involved in writing a book.

Just like bobsledding, the process of getting my story organized and transferred from my head to the book you now hold was a team effort. I couldn't have done it without the help and support of great friends and family who were with me every step of the way.

First, my mom and dad remain my biggest fans and strongest supporters. Even during my darkest hours, their love and guidance remained with me. I am truly thankful for everything they have done.

Also, my sisters, Megan Holcomb and Stephanie Petersen, and my brother-in-law, Eric Petersen, have been faithful supporters and, more importantly, great friends throughout.

Of course, a great note of thanks goes to Justin Olsen, Steve Mesler, Curt Tomasevicz, and all of my USBSF teammates, as well as my coach and friend Brian Shimer, without whom our accomplishments would have never been possible.

Geoff Bodine was kind enough to share his personal story for this book, helping me to understand his history in bobsledding and the development and future of the Bo-Dyn Bobsled Project. None of us in bobsledding can thank Geoff and his team enough.

Dr. Brian Boxer Wachler was also extremely generous with his time, jarring my memory and educating me even further on the science behind the procedure that now bears my name. Many thanks, friend. I owe you everything.

And, of course, a great note of thanks to all my friends who stuck with me through thick and thin in my career and in life: Tristan Gale-Geisler, Katie Uhlaender, Kristy Lees Shields, and my friend and agent Brant Feldman of American Group Management; Kevin Plank, Tori Hanna, Kevin Culley, and the entire Under Armour team; Rob Graf and the Advocare family; Darrin Steele and the United States Bobsled and Skeleton Federation, as well as the USOC, and the Olympic Training Center staffs at Lake Placid, Colorado Springs, and Chula Vista.

Being new to the literary world, I was shepherded through the process by a great team of professionals, including Steve Troha of Folio Literary Management, my coauthor Steve Eubanks, my editor Debbie Harmsen, and the entire staff of BenBella Books.

A warm and heartfelt thanks to you all.